The Best Mac Tips Ever

Steve Michel and Dale Coleman

Osborne **McGraw-Hill**

Berkeley   New York   St. Louis   San Francisco
Auckland   Bogotá   Hamburg   London   Madrid
Mexico City   Milan   Montreal   New Delhi   Panama City
Paris   São Paulo   Singapore   Sydney
Tokyo   Toronto

Osborne **McGraw-Hill**
2600 Tenth Street
Berkeley, California 94710
U.S.A.

For information on translations or book distributors outside of the U.S.A., please write to Osborne **McGraw-Hill** at the above address.

The Best Mac Tips Ever

1234567890 DOC 9987654

ISBN 0-07-881968-7

The Best Mac
Tips Ever

Steve:

To Margaret, Lyal, Richard, and Genevieve Michel

Dale:

To Barry Austin and the entire Quintara Street gang

Table of Contents

Table of Contents

2 Other System Software

3 Printing and Fonts

4
Networks and Communication

5
System Tips

Tip

6
Generic Application Tips

7
Healthy Computing

8
PowerBook Tips

A
Glossary

B
Resources

Index

Acknowledgments

These tips were compiled from a variety of sources, but primarily from our own experience using the Mac. Any mistakes you find here are solely our responsibility; we've yet to discover the magic keyboard equivalent for the hidden perfection command. Any book is a group project, and those involved with this one have earned our respect and gratitude. Specifically, we want to thank our stern taskmasters Frances Stack, Jeff Pepper, and Bob Myren, and our stalwartly tech editor Bob Kermish. Others we relied on for one critical thing or another include Xavier Raya, Keith Quirollo, Mick and Laurie McCuistion, David Todd, Craig O'Donnell, Michael Britten, Chiqui Linda, Carol Corolla, Barry Austin, Mia Runanin, Maria Sample, Paul Smethers of Central Point Software, David Methven of DayStar Digital, and Boingo Boingo, who make the best cafe mocha in San Francisco.

Introduction

The Macintosh is a paradox. On the one hand, almost anyone with a minim of motivation can use it with almost no understanding of how things work. Those who use a spreadsheet for all their word processing tasks fall into this category. On the other hand, anyone so inclined can fritter away the best years of their life in Mac minutiae in the course of becoming the ultimate power user. These folks are perhaps best left unidentified.

Between these two extremes are those of us who have real work to do. For us, buying and learning to use a Mac is the best productivity investment we've ever made. If you already have a life, you probably don't want to devote it to getting the most out of your Mac. But you use a Mac regularly and probably wouldn't mind knowing a trick or two to make your work time more efficient. If so, this book is for you.

Together, we have nearly 20 years experience with the Macintosh—just about as much experience as any two users can have. We remember the excitement when we first saw the Mac and got our own—at last a computer you could use without having to memorize arcane commands, and we hoped, one that you could use without having to resort to documentation. What a lofty goal.

Unfortunately, but probably predictably, the Mac has become much more complex over the last couple of years. Both Apple and third party developers have added all sorts of facilities to the system that end up making it much more complex than it used to be. And despite the fact that Apple's documentation is in general very good, we find that not everyone reads it. Perhaps that's the paradox of the system: it seems so simple on the surface that you might not realize that there are hidden wonders waiting for you if you peek just below the surface. That was one of our goals in producing this book: to reveal some of the Mac's capabilities that may escape those who haven't looked below the surface.

Another goal of this book has been to show you some of the consequences of some features, and some good standard ways to use facilities. For example, we rely heavily on aliases to make all kinds of files and folders easy to get at, and present a few ways to go about this.

With those goals in mind, we wrote these tips primarily for those who already know something about the Mac. We've stayed away from tips that work only if you are using a certain program, or a certain combination of programs.

We've stayed away from dealing with the basics: how to use the mouse, how to turn the machine on, and how to type. Instead, we've tried to show you how to use your basic knowledge in the most efficient ways possible.

One of our goals was to recommend public domain, freeware, and shareware utilities as often as possible. Sometimes it seems as if you can find a freely available program to solve nearly any problem you need to solve; very often these are more useful and of better quality than are commercial equivalents. All serious Mac users should attempt to connect to one or more reliable sources of this kind of software, such as a user group, commercial online service, bulletin board service, a well-connected friend, or whatever. What's really important to remember is that when an author asks for money in return for a program, you pay up; that's what encourages software authors to create more.

Over the next couple of years, the face of the Mac will probably change a great deal. The transition to the new PowerPC chip, new versions of the operating system, and strange capabilities of new devices such as the Newton will change the way we use our Macs. A firm foundation in doing things right right now will make this transition easier. We hope we can update this book as time goes on, to help you make this transition.

How to Use This Book

This book is designed to be a reference, although you may be tempted to read it from cover to cover solely for the majesty of its prose. If you're looking for information about a specific topic, the best place to start is the index, which points to the individual tips related to that entry. If you come across a word or phrase that has no meaning in the real world, turn to the glossary. We tried to include in the glossary all the jargon that we used in the book.

The tips are numbered and grouped together in broad categories. So if you're curious about a general topic such as printing or system software, you can browse the part dealing with that subject.

Each tip is also written to be complete (a stand-alone product, if you will). But often related tips and subjects are near by. We assume that you're as busy as we are, so we try to make each tip as concise as possible. In this case, we believe that conciseness is the ultimate virtue.

Finally, we mention many products from many companies and individuals. Contact information is contained in Appendix B. You'll find listings for each product by product name, plus entries for each company.

Finder Tips

The Finder is the core of the Macintosh, the most important Mac program you use. This first section gives you tips that can help make it easier for you to get to the files and application programs you use most often.

TIP 1 Selecting Icons

There are several ways to select icons in the Finder. Of course, you can select an icon by simply clicking once on it; when it highlights, it is selected. Use the SHIFT key to select multiple icons by clicking on them.

If you want to select several adjacent icons, click and hold the mouse button near the icons and drag to create a rectangle enclosing the icons, as shown here:

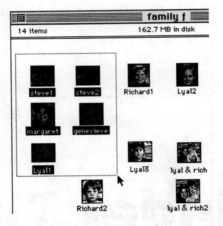

The icons will select *as you drag the rectangle around them.*

You can use a combination of techniques to select files that aren't adjacent. After selecting a number of files, you can hold down the SHIFT key while selecting more files, and the new files are added to the selected set.

In list views, you can also drag to select icons, as shown here:

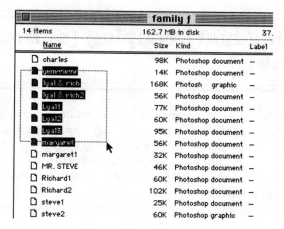

Note that in list views, the Finder leaves a margin at the left edge of the window to give you room to drag. You can also start the drag to the right of the filenames.

Remember that list views and their outline capabilities make it easy to select files that are in separate folders: in this illustration, the file named "template" was first selected; then the SHIFT key was held down while dragging to select the separate group of files in the folder (which was expanded).

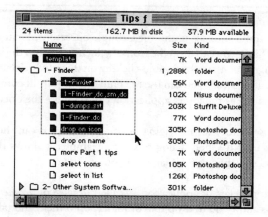

Dragging and Dropping (or Drop Till You Bop)

One of the essential Mac techniques is dragging and dropping. Prior to System 7, there were three classes of objects onto which you could drop files: disks (for copying files to different disks), folders (for moving them into different folders), and the trash (for deleting files). Beyond these types of containers for objects, System 7 extends this drag-and-drop ability to two other classes of objects. The first is applications: a document can be dropped on top of an application, which opens the application and tells it to open the dropped document. The second class is the System Folder; certain kinds of items, when dropped on the System folder, are placed in specific locations within that folder (and these are discussed in Part 5).

The Benefits of Opening Files with Drag and Drop

Dropping documents onto applications is useful for a couple of reasons. First, it makes the Finder a useful tool for opening files. Since you can drop the icon of a document onto the icon of an application, you are not limited to opening documents by double-clicking on them (which launches the application that created the document). This means you can use the Finder to import documents into applications that did not create them (as long as the target application can translate the document).

The Finder is also a more useful tool for managing documents, since it can show more information about them than can the standard Open dialog box. For example, it shows the date and time the document was modified and can show Finder labels, if you use them.

This capability has led to a new class of applications—called *droplets* or *grinders* (depending on who you are talking to). Droplets allow you to drop files or folders onto them and take the same action on all the dropped items. For example, Leonard Rosenthol's DTPrinter is an application that creates droplets that correspond to different printers on the network; you can print a specific document on a specific printer by dropping that document's icon on top of DTPrinter's icon.

How to Drag and Drop

Dragging and dropping icons is a basic Macintosh technique: simply click (once) the icon of the document you want to open and, while keeping the mouse button held down, move the mouse pointer until you are pointing at the icon of the application you want to use to open the document. When the icon of the application becomes highlighted, release the mouse button, and the document is opened in that application. The following illustration shows the icon of a Nisus document being dropped onto the icon of Microsoft Word. Since Nisus creates text documents, Word can open them.

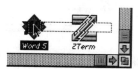

The standard icon view is the best view to use for windows containing icons you will use as targets for dropping; its larger icons (than the small icon view) are easy to hit. However, list views (any of those that are shown when you use one of the non-icon views on the View menu) also work with drag and drop. As shown next, the name of an application highlights when you pass the mouse pointer over any area in the list view that contains printing. That is, you don't need to hit the very small icon, or even the name of the application, but can drop the icon on the text containing the icon's size or kind information.

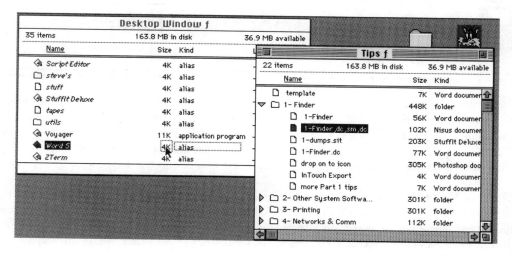

By the way, Apple's forthcoming Apple Open Collaboration Environment (AOCE), due for release in late 1993, changes (yet again) drag and drop. While we haven't tested it, we understand that the Finder that comes as part of AOCE will allow you to drag icons from the Finder into open windows that are part of applications.

When Dropping Icons, Remember That the Item That Highlights Is the Target for the Dropped Icon

When dropping an icon into an open window, remember that if an icon in that window highlights, then that icon (whether it's a folder or an application) becomes the target for that dropped file. The only time this becomes a problem is when the window contains a *list* of other folders. If you want to place the file into one of these folders, that's easy to do. However, if you want instead to drop the icon into the same level as the other folders, it can be a little tricky. There are two solutions. First, you can drop the icon into an empty space *below* the list of icons, or you can drop it into the header information for the window (the area just below the title bar).

About Mac Memory and Memory Fragmentation

Memory, also called RAM, is the location into which applications and documents are loaded when you open them. As you open and close applications, especially if you are in the habit of having several applications open at a time (a good habit, by the way), the Mac's memory can become *fragmented*. That is, you can reach a situation in which you have enough free memory to open another application, but that memory might not be contiguous. Here's an example of how that happens.

When the Mac starts, a certain portion of its memory is used for System functions. This includes the memory used by the System itself, the various control panels and extensions you have installed, and the Finder. This allocated System memory is labeled System Software in the About This Macintosh display. The following three charts represent all the memory in a 4Mb Macintosh. In this graphic, no software other than the System is running:

> System

System Software, in this example, occupies about half (2MB) of the total 4Mb available. In the following graphic, two applications are opened: Application A uses about 500K of memory and Application B uses about 1Mb of memory:

> System   A   B

With both these applications open, About This Macintosh reports that the largest unused block is about 500K. But suppose you want to run a third application, which requires about 1Mb of RAM. You might surmise that you need to quit Appliation A to free the additional RAM (the 500K used by Application A and the 500K already available add up to 1Mb). While quitting Application A does indeed return the memory it uses to the available total, the memory is fragmented, as shown here:

> System   B

The free space left by Application A is not contiguous to the other block of free space, so the About This Mac display still shows only 500K free. The only way to free this memory is to quit Appliction B as well.

There's no real way to prevent this from happening. You can be careful about the order in which you start your applications, opening those that require the most memory first. If you encounter this situation more than occasionally, the only real solution is to install more memory. In this example, if 8Mb of memory were available, the user could have all three applications open at the same time.

Back Up Files Well and Often

T^{IP} 7

Back up your files. If you're not doing this already, this sage advice is probably rolling off your back as you read. But when the day inevitably comes that your entire disk drive goes south, or you inadvertently delete the file containing the report on which your entire career-advancement scheme hinges, we, at least, will still sleep the quiet sleep of the righteous.

We use Dantz DiskFit to perform a complete backup of each of our disk drives to removable-cartridge drives at least once a week. We back up certain in-progress files, such as the chapters of this book, almost hourly. There are other good utilities available, such as Fifth Generation FastBack, Dantz Retrospect, and backup programs in both the Norton Utilities and Central Point MacTools. But what really matters is the task, not which tool you use to perform it. Any functional backup utility is better than none. When comparing backup programs, choose one that you find easy to use since the easier it is to use, the more likely you are to actually use it.

Save Early and Often

Related to the backup question is the question of saving documents that you are working on. Save at regular intervals while you are working. Even with large files on slow disk drives, the few seconds delay you might experience while the file is being written to disk is nothing compared to the frustration you will certainly experience if your Mac crashes or freezes exactly two sweat-drenched hours after your last save.

Save Files to Separate Locations as You Work with Them

Even while you are working on a file, it's a good idea to save the file you are working on to a separate location—either to a separate volume, such as floppy or network disk, or even to a separate folder. If a crash or freeze occurs, work in memory can be lost, but some programs that constantly write changes to files can have those files corrupted; FileMaker Pro is an example of this (though it's pretty good about recovering corrupted files). Some programs, such as Nisus and MacWrite Pro, let you specify separate locations where backup files are kept, and files are saved there automatically each time you use the Save command. Microsoft Word lets you save a backup file, which does not change the location of the original file you are saving. See Tip 12 about the dangers of using the Save As command as a method of keeping a backup of a work in progress.

Keep Several Sets of Backups

A strange fact of backing up is that most of the media to which we back up are less reliable than hard disks. This is true of backing up to floppy disk, to most cartridges, and even to tape (though less so of magneto-optical cartridges and tape). That's an excellent reason to keep several sets of backups. The more copies of something you have, the less likely it is that *all* of them will go bad at once. We rotate two sets of backups, alternating between weeks.

Keep One Set of Backups Off Site

Computer disasters causing loss of data aren't the only reason to back up files. Fires, floods, robberies, and other events mandated by God and Murphy are all good reasons to maintain backups. Consider that if your backups are kept at the same location as your computer, chances are such a disaster that affects one (your computer) will affect them all. Insurance policies can replace hardware, but they can't replace data. That's why it's a good idea to keep a set of backups at a different locations. For example, you might store backups of your home system at your office and vice versa, assuming your employer allows it. Safe deposit boxes have their own special appeal for the those who are sufficiently paranoid.

Why Using Save As to Save to a Different Volume (Such as a Floppy Disk or Secondary Hard Disk) Isn't Such a Hot Idea

Making frequent backups of important files to another volume such as a floppy disk or a secondary hard drive as you work on them is both wise and prudent. However, using your application's Save As command to save to another volume can lead to a lot of confusion. You're much better off to use the Finder to drag a copy of the file from the hard disk to a floppy. If you use the Save As command instead, the new location becomes the default for the file, so the next time you use the Save command, the file is saved to this new location. As a result, it's far too easy to become completely confused about which volume has the most up-to-date copy.

Instead, when saving to a floppy disk in the middle of some work, switch to the Finder (closing the file if necessary) and use the Finder to copy the file to an alternative location.

Why Rebuilding the Desktop at Least Once a Month Makes Sense

The Finder automatically maintains two invisible files at the top level of each volume. These two files, named Desktop DB and Desktop DF, are together called *the Desktop*. The Finder uses these files to store information about each file on that volume, such as its icon and, if the file is created by an application, the name of the application that created it. As you use a volume, adding and deleting document and application files, the Desktop becomes less efficient and sometimes becomes corrupted. This usually results in sluggish disk performance and, if the Desktop is corrupted, errors when you attempt to open a file. The solution is to *rebuild* the Desktop.

Rebuilding the Desktop can take several minutes or longer, depending on the size of the volume and the number of files and applications involved.

Use Get Info Comments with Caution Because They Are Lost When You Rebuild the Desktop

When the desktop is rebuilt, all Get Info comments are discarded, which is why using the Get Info comments feature is a waste of time in most cases. The desktop should be rebuilt at least every month or so (see Tip 13), so if you use Get Info comments to, say, add comments to a file you're sharing with a coworker, keep this limitation of the Finder in mind. Apple promised to rectify this annoying situation with System 7 back in 1989, but failed to deliver.

How to Rebuild the Desktop

The standard way to rebuild the Desktop is to press simultaneously the ⌘ and OPTION keys as the Finder mounts the volume. Volumes mount as part of the startup process. Floppy disks and other removable media such as Syquest, Bernoulli and magneto-optical cartridges are also volumes, and they mount when you insert them into their drive. You can rebuild the desktop on these volumes by using the same ⌘-OPTION key technique when you insert them.

Another way to rebuild the desktop, more automatic than the standard way, is to save a file called "desktop" (exactly that name, no spaces) at the top level of the disk on which you want the desktop to be rebuilt. The next time you start your machine, the Finder will see this file, and mistake it for the older file, named "Desktop," that System 6 used. Thinking that the disk was used by System 6, and noting that the new file is newer than its own Desktop DB and Desktop DF files, the Finder will automatically rebuild those files. On subsequent restarts, the Finder will not rebuild the desktop, as the two new files are newer than the "desktop" file.

You Can't Rebuild the Desktop File on Empty Floppies

When you use a floppy disk repeatedly to hold a number of different kinds of files (perhaps, when you copy files from the office to work on at home), the invisible desktop files on the floppy can become quite large, often to the point of reducing their storage capacity. In this illustration, even though the floppy holds no files, its desktop files take up 36K of disk space:

To recover the space occupied by this generally useless (to you) information, rebuild the desktop on the floppy (by holding down the ⌘ and OPTION keys when you insert the floppy).

However, the desktop files of a floppy disk *cannot* be rebuilt if there are no files on the disk. The Finder doesn't warn you of this fact, but instead ignores your request to rebuild the desktop.

There are two ways to remedy this situation. First, you can save a small file on the empty floppy, rebuild the desktop, and trash the small file. (Creating a new folder rather than a file works just as well and is often more convenient.) In the following illustration, rebuilding the desktop and deleting the file has reduced the size of the desktop file to 1K.

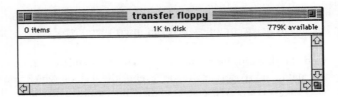

You can also use the Finder's Erase Disk command on the floppy. This has the disadvantage of taking longer than rebuilding the desktop, but has the advantage of verifying the integrity of the disk.

Avoid Completely Filling Your Hard Disk

It's easy enough to fill up even the largest hard disks, but it's a good idea to leave 2Mb to 5Mb of free space, and more on larger disks. The free space is put to good use when you install new software that needs additional temporary space to complete the installation process. Also, some applications need space for a temporary file or files when running. In addition, some applications have difficulty when they are asked to save a file to a volume that doesn't have enough free space available and, in such situations, tend to bomb.

For example, PhotoShop uses its own virtual memory scheme, and so needs to have plenty of free disk space (about three times the size of the file you're working on). If you're working with a document held in memory and it becomes larger than the available free disk space, you won't be able to save unless you have another volume available with enough free space.

How to Display the Space Available on a Volume in Folder Windows

A quick way to see the amount of space used and the amount of space free on a volume is to tell the Finder to display that information at the top of windows just below the title bar. This area is called the "header." To use this feature, open the Views control panel, and check the box called Show Disk Info. In addition to space used and space free on the volume, checking this box also tells the Finder to display the numbers of items in the folder.

Use a Folder Window to Monitor Free Disk Space

If you frequently need to monitor how much space is available on a volume, you can switch to the Finder and look at any folder window if you've checked Show Disk Info in the Views control panel. If you don't want to bother with switching to the Finder, you can easily make a dedicated folder to display current disk space information at the bottom of your screen.

Create a new folder on the volume you want to monitor. Give it a meaningful name, such as the same name as the volume or "Free space monitor." Open the folder, and make the window as small as you can while still displaying the size information. Now position the window at the bottom of the screen so that just the window header information is visible, like this:

If you make such folders for each volume you use, keep them open, and if you resize the windows of other applications so they don't use the bottom portion of the screen, you will always have a monitor of how much space is left on all the disks you use. This tip is particularly useful if you regularly deal with floppy disks that are nearly full.

If the available free space information is not visible in the folder you create, make sure the Show Disk Info in Header box in the Views control panel is checked.

How Many Volumes, Files, and Folders Can the Mac Support?

Although it's unlikely you'll run into any of them (at least in the short term), there *are* limits to the Mac file system; it can hold only so many files and folders. Here's the rundown:

❑ The maximum size of a single volume is 2Gb (2,000 Mb). Manufacturers are already supplying some lucky customers with drives that large and larger. But larger capacity drives will be available. (Drives can be divided into logical divisions called partitions.)

❏ The largest a file can be, coincidentally, is also 2Gb.

❏ There is no hard-wired limit as to how many volumes can be mounted at once, except for memory. When a new volume is mounted, the Finder requires more memory to hold information about that volume, and the system heap grows (but not by much).

❏ The maximum number of files and folders on a volume is 65,535 (which is 2^{16}). Should you need more than this on a single disk, the best solution is to partition the disk into separate volumes.

❏ The maximum number of files in a folder is 32,768 (2^{15}). However, it's better to avoid this limit, as the Finder slows significantly when dealing with an enormously large number of files, and the routines used for displaying filenames inside Open File dialogs cannot work with more than about 900 files. (We can't be more specific about the exact number because it is affected by the length of filenames; usually the limit will be closer to 800 files.)

Use the File Menu's Put Away Command to Eject Disks

While there's something satisfying about dragging a volume to the trash to remove it from the desktop, doing so can cause a flutter in the hearts of those new to the Mac. Instead, select the disk you want to eject, then use the Finder File menu Put Away command to eject disks and remove their icons. This has a second benefit: if the item you are dragging to the trash is *not* a volume (a possibility if you're using custom icons), files that you mistake for volumes won't be inadvertently erased if you use the Put Away command rather than dragging the icon to the Trash.

Catalog Files on Floppy Disks with Aliases for Quick Access

One slick use of aliases is to use them to create a quick, on-the-fly floppy disk catalog. Follow these steps to create a folder on your boot volume that contains aliases of files stored on floppy disks.

1. Create a folder on the desktop and give it a meaningful name, such as Aliases of Floppy Files. Place it on the desktop so it's easy to access.

2. Lock the labeled floppy disk you want to catalog.

3. Insert the first disk you want to catalog in the floppy drive and open it.

4. Select the file or files you want to alias.

5. Choose the Make Alias command on the Finder's File menu. Since the floppy disk is locked, the Finder cannot create new alias files on that disk. Instead, it summons a dialog box that asks you if want the aliases saved to the Desktop. Click the OK button in this dialog box.

6. The Finder creates an alias for each file you've selected on the Desktop. Note that since all the alias files are selected, you can drag them as a group into your new alias folder in one step.

7. Repeat steps 2 through 6 for each floppy disk you want to catalog.

With this technique, you are freed from having to remember which floppy disk contains which file. When you double-click the alias of the file, the Finder asks you to insert the proper floppy disk by name.

You can also use the Get Info command on the alias file, and use the Find Original button in the Get Info window to have the Finder prompt you for the disk.

This technique is useful only if you actually label your floppy disks with the same name that the Finder uses.

Use the Finder's Duplicate Command to Create a Safe Backup Before You Edit a Critical File

TIP 23

Occasionally you might edit a critically important file, only to discover that you've made a complete mess and were better off with the original. If you can imagine this happening to you, before you open the file, make a copy of it with the Finder's File menu Duplicate command. As an added precaution, you can also use the Get Info window to lock the copy. This way, you can edit the original to your heart's content without the fuss and bother of pointless paranoia.

Almost Everyone Can Use Stationery Pad Documents

Many users completely overlook the handy System 7 Stationery Pad feature. You can create a stationery pad file by clicking the Stationery Pad check box in the file's Get Info window. When you open a Stationery Pad file, the Finder automatically summons the Save As dialog box, which prompts you to give a name to the file you have created, leaving the original file intact for use another day.

Some applications directly support stationery files. Those applications will automatically open the file in an Untitled window. If you open a Stationery Pad file for an application that does not support stationery, the Finder summons this dialog box:

> **You have opened a stationery pad, so a new document will be created.**
>
> **Type a name for the new document:**
>
> `100 Top Objects copy`
>
> [Save In...]   [Cancel]   [**OK**]

This lets you specify a name and location for the new file. When you click the OK button, the Finder creates a copy of the file in that location and with that name and then opens that file with the application.

Stationery Pad files are useful for such things as letterheads and memo forms. You can also use for it any documents that serve as templates: standard spreadsheets, graphics files, and even for databases for which you want to have an audit trail.

Which Version of an Application is Launched When You Have More Than One Version of It on a Mounted Volume?

If you have more than one version of an application on your hard disk (in different folders, or the same application with different names), when you double-click on an document created by that application, the Finder launches the one with the more recent creation or modification date. Normally, you should have only one version of an application on a disk, since multiple versions can lead to complications with ancillary files such as Preferences files. However, occasionally it's comforting when upgrading to keep the older one around until you get fully acquainted with the new version. In this case, before you install the new version, lock and store the Preference file of the older version in a different location on disk.

How to Force the Finder to Launch the Older Version of an Application

While the Finder automatically launches the newer of two versions of the same application when you open a document file, System 7 provides a simple mechanism to force it to launch the older one instead. To do so, drag and drop the icon of the document file on the icon of the older version of the application.

Use ⌘-. to Cancel Operations

The ⌘-. key combination is the standard "Cancel" command on the Mac (DOS users will see this as the rough equivalent of CTRL-C, or more commonly, CTRL-BREAK). It will halt many, if not all, operations once they have started. The ESC key often performs the same function as ⌘-.

Sometimes You Can Use ⌘-OPTION-ESC to Exit from a Frozen Application; Sometimes You Can't

The three-fingered ⌘-OPTION-ESC key combination will sometimes let you escape from an application when it freezes. It doesn't always work, but it does work often enough that it's handy to remember it. When an application freezes, it usually takes the entire system with it, in which case you have to press the programmer reset switch (the one on the left with the small triangle above it) to restart your Mac. When the ⌘-OPTION-ESC sequence works, it summons a dialog box asking if you really want to quit the application. Click OK, and the frozen application quits and returns you to the Finder Desktop. Rather than continue working, save all open documents in any other applications that are running and use the Special menu's Restart command. Restarting helps ensure that anything that might have gone awry with the system to cause the freeze is corrected.

Note that sometimes you don't have to be quick to jump the gun with the ⌘-OPTION-ESC sequence. Sometimes an application appears to be frozen, but isn't really, and returns control back to you after a minute or two. We encountered this situation when we used to run large, demanding applications on slower Macs. Adobe PhotoShop on a stock Mac SE is an example.

The Graceful Way to Restart after a Hang or a Freeze

Since the Mac hangs from time to time, it's prudent to know how to restart. You can restart with a quick flip of the power switch, but this isn't recommended, as it stresses the Mac's electronics unnecessarily. You're much better off pressing the programmer's reset switch. There are so many differently configured Macs available that it's no longer possible to tell you where your Mac's programmer reset switch is. Instead, consult your Mac manual.

Use Aliases to Make Files Appear to Be in Several Places at Once

Aliases are one of the best features of System 7. You can create an alias for a file, a folder or a volume. An alias file is a small (usually less than 600 bytes) file that contains pointers to the original. You can use alias files to make their originals appear to be in more than just one place. For example, you might use a spreadsheet file in several ongoing projects. If you group your files in folders by project (often an excellent technique, by the way), you can place an alias of the spreadsheet file in each project folder. As far as applications are concerned, aliases function just like the original. For example, alias files appear in Open dialog box lists, and selecting an alias file causes the application to open the original file. Also, double-clicking an alias of a file opens its original (sometimes called the *parent* of the alias).

How to Make an Alias File

To make an alias, select the file (or folder or volume), then use the Finder's File menu Make Alias command. This instructs the Finder to create a second file with the same name as the original (with the word "alias" appended to it). The filename of the alias file appears in italics. You can then move this alias file to another location.

How to Ensure That Your Operations Affect the Original File and Not Its Alias

Only opening an alias affects the original and not the alias file itself. Other common operations, such as dragging the icon to the trash or copying it affects only the alias file itself and not the original.

This means that when you copy a file to a floppy disk (perhaps for sharing with others) you have to make sure to copy the file itself and not its alias. Otherwise, the person to whom you give the file will not be able to open the file, but will be greeted with this dialog box instead:

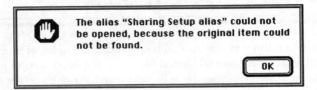

TIP 33

How to Locate Quickly the Original of an Alias File

The more you use aliases, the harder it is to keep track of the exact location of each one's original file. Fortunately, the Finder gives you a method to navigate to the original quickly. Select an alias and then use the Finder's Get Info command. The window it produces is shown here:

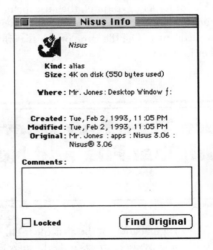

The Get Info window contains a Find Original button. If you click this button, the finder opens the folder containing the original and highlights the original.

What Does an Alias File Actually Store?

Each alias file contains several pieces of information about the original file, folder, or volume. First, it contains a full *path* to the original (a path is a listing of all the containers of the file, in this form: *Hard Disk name:folder name:folder name: filename*). This information is displayed in the portion of the Get Info window of an alias labeled "Original."

When you attempt to open an alias, or when you use the Find Original button in the alias' Get Info window, the Finder first checks in the specified location to see if the original is there. If it's not, it then uses the ID reference number to find the original. The operating system assigns an ID reference number to a file or folder when it is first created; the ID number remains unchanged for the life of the file or folder. This way, the Finder can still find an alias' original, even if the original has been moved.

An alias stays connected to its original as long as either one of these two pieces of information is valid.

Copying a File or Files to an Alias of a Folder or Volume

If the original of an alias is of a folder or volume, dragging files to that alias, is the same as dragging the files to the icon of that volume or folder.

Can You Move the Parent of an Aliased File?

Because the alias file stores the original's File ID, you can move the original of an alias to a different location on the same disk, and the original can still be found when it's needed.

However, you *cannot* move the original of an alias to a different volume and still have the alias connected. The reason for this is that when you move a file to a different volume, The Finder actually creates a new file. This copy has its own unique File ID and path name. When you delete the original (as the last part of the move), the original of the parent is actually gone.

Can You Replace the Original (Parent) of an Aliased File?

You can replace the original (parent) of an alias file and retain the connection with the alias, only if you give the replacement file exactly the same name, and place it in the same folder.

Keep Aliases Connected When You Upgrade to a New Version of an Application by Removing the Version Number from the Name

If you keep aliases of frequently used applications in the Apple Menu Items folder or if you use the technique described in Tip 44 to create a folder for aliases of applications, you can still maintain the links to the originals. You only have to remember to make sure the new original has the same name as the old original and is in the same location.

In most cases this means removing the version number from the application filenames. When we install new software, we immediately remove the version number from the filename. We do the same when we install an upgraded version. This way any alias of the application stays linked to the application. Some vendors, such as Microsoft, usually omit version numbers from filenames.

You Can Access Anything That Has an Icon from the Apple Menu

It's easy to miss one of the easiest ways to customize the Finder to reflect the way you work. It's called the Apple menu, and System 7 gives you an easy way to add to it any item that has an icon: desk accessories; files; folders; and aliases of files, folders, and volumes. Everything that appears on the Apple menu is stored in a folder, in the top level of the System Folder, called Apple Menu Items. For example, if you're going to be working on a specific file for several days or even weeks, put it in the Apple Menu Items folder. It will then never be more than a menu command away, and you won't have to dig through nested folders to open it. Aliases of these items make even more sense in the Apple Menus Items folder, since they are very small and won't bloat your System Folder.

Mounting a Remote Volume with an Alias

Mounting a remote network volume with the Chooser is a bit too complicated for everyday use. Instead, create an alias of the remote volume. Then when you want to mount the remote volume, just double-click the alias. Depending on whether or not you have told AppleShare to save your name and password, the remote volume will either mount automatically or the AppleShare dialog asking for your name and password will appear. Either way, it's a lot more convenient than dealing with the Chooser.

Mounting a Remote Volume and Opening a Folder on It in One Step

Just as you can mount a remote volume with an alias of that volume (see Tip 40), you can mount a remote volume by opening an alias of a folder on that volume. If you have instructed AppleShare to save your name and password, you can use this technique to mount the remote volume and open the original folder in one action. If not, you'll have to give AppleShare your name and password, but then the remote volume will mount and the specified folder will open.

Place an Alias of the Apple Menu Items Folder in the Apple Menu Items Folder

If you find that you add and remove items from the Apple menu frequently, you may find it convenient to put an alias of the Apple Menu Items folder itself in the Apple Menu Items folder. Open the System Folder, select the Apple Menu Items folder, choose the Make Alias command. Next, drag that alias into the Apple Menu Items folder. With this technique, you can quickly and easily open the Apple Menu Items folder by selecting it from the Apple Menu.

Place Aliases of Folders That You Access Frequently in the Apple Menu Items Folder

Any folder that you access more than once or twice a week deserves a place on the Apple menu. You can also place aliases of other items that you open often, such as the System Folder. Likely candidates for this treatment include the Fonts folder and the Extensions folder, which can have aliases placed in the Apple Menu Items folder.

Place Aliases of Frequently Used Applications, Files, and Folders on the Desktop or in a Folder on the Desktop

As nifty as the Apple menu is, scrolling through a long list of items can get tedious. For quick access to the most commonly used items, we use a special folder we call the Desktop Window folder that we keep open on the desktop most of the time. (We could call it the Bob folder, but we like to give folders descriptive names.) This folder resides on our desktop, and contains aliases of applications, files, and folders that we use often.

Placing the folder on the desktop makes it easy to get to. We adopted two other techniques that make it easy to manage:

❑ We place an alias of the folder in the Apple Menu Items folder and precede its name there with a space, which puts it at the top menu. Then we can access it easily, even when an application is active (with the Finder hidden in the background).

❑ We place an alias of the Desktop Window folder in the Startup Items folder. This means that after every restart, it is opened on our desktop.

Here for example are Dale's and Steve's Desktop Windows:

 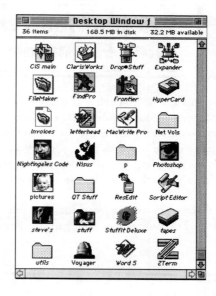

These two examples give you an idea of the kinds of files or aliases that you can place into these windows.

TIP 45

How to Keep the Apple Menu Available

When the Apple menu is longer than your monitor can display at one time, scrolling to the items at the end of the menu can quickly become tedious, particularly if you're using one of the slower Macs such as the Classic. Since the items on the menu are really files in the Apple Menu folder, you might find it convenient to keep the folder open on the desktop at all times.

Put an alias of the Apple Menu Items folder itself in the Apple Menu Items folder so that it appears on the menu. This gives you a quick way to open it and keep it open, no matter what application you're using at the time. If you want the Apple Menu Items folder to open every time you start up your Mac, place an alias of it in the System folder Startup Items folder.

TIP 46

You Can Take the "Alias" Out of Your Alias Filename

Each time you make an alias of a file, the Finder automatically appends the word "alias" to the new alias filename. You can safely delete the alias from the end of the name. The only thing to remember is that you must first move the alias to a different folder from the original file. Even though the names of aliases appear in italics, the Finder acts as if it can't make the distinction between italic and regular type, and complains that you're attempting to create two files with the same name if you try to remove the "alias" from the alias filename without moving it to another folder first.

For that matter, you can rename an alias file to just about any legal filename. Although this can lead to a great deal of confusion on your part, the Finder will remember the name of the original file just fine.

TIP 47

Where Do Alias Files Get Their Icons?

You can assign custom icons to aliases to make them look any way you want. Otherwise, an alias file gets its icon from its original. The alias gets its icon when it is created. If the icon of the original changes (that is, if you assign it a custom icon), the icon of the alias is not changed until the desktop is rebuilt.

Use the Pop-Up on a Finder Window to Determine Its Location on the Volume

Here's a System 7 feature that a lot of reasonably competent and knowledgeable users have missed: The name of each folder, as it's displayed in the title bar of the open folder window, is actually a pop-up menu that works exactly like the navigation pop-up menu in the standard Open and Save dialog boxes. This pop-up menu shows the names of the folders of that top folder of the directory.

To activate this menu, hold down the ⌘ key while pressing the mouse button on the window name. This displays the path, as shown here:

You can navigate to any folder on the pop-up menu by dragging to its name. You can navigate to one of these other folders and simultaneously close the currently open folder by holding down the Option key when you release the mouse button.

This tip is particularly handy after you have used the Finder Find File command to locate a file or folder. When Find File locates a file or folder, it opens the folder that contains it, and leaves the found item selected. If you don't recognize the name of the folder (and it can be hard to remember where many of them are if you have a lot of folders), you can use this technique to see the path.

Use the OPTION Key to Close a Window When You Open Something That's in It

If you hold down the OPTION key when you open something in a Finder window, the window that contains that item is automatically closed. This works whether you are opening a folder or file. If it's a file, then the window closes after the application has launched (you see it zoom closed behind the application).

How to Close All Open Windows with the Hidden Close All Command

In the Finder when you hold down the OPTION key, the Finder File menu's Close command changes to Close All. This hidden Close All command closes all the open windows on your desktop. The keyboard equivalent of the Close command is ⌘-W; the keyboard equivalent of the Close All command is OPTION-⌘-W.

This technique, by the way, works in all Mac applications that follow Apple's guidelines. (Many popular applications, including Microsoft Word and AppleTalk Remote Access don't fall into this category.) If data in any window hasn't been saved, you are prompted to save before the window closes. Some applications (such as HyperCard) cannot run with no windows open, so the final window will not be closed when you use the Close All command.

Icon Views versus List Views

Finder windows can have two general kinds of views: icon views (in either large or small sizes) and list views (which include the various methods of sorting the lists). Each kind of view has its own strengths and weaknesses.

Icon views are useful for folders that have few items in them—we find that the limit is about two dozen items. Icon views are also useful when the items in a folder have different icons (either because they are different applications or are files created by different applications); it doesn't make much sense, for example, to use icon views when a folder contains a couple dozen Microsoft Word document icons whose only distinguishing feature is the name. Icon views also have the advantage of including the disk's capacity and free space at the top of the window.

List views, by the same token, are more useful when the contents of a folder grow beyond a couple dozen items, and when the contents are otherwise homogeneous. In that same example of a folder full of Word documents, you're usually more interested in the file's name than its appearance.

Use the OPTION Key with the Clean Up Command to Order Icons in a Window

If you hold down the OPTION key while clicking on the Finder's Special menu, you will see that the name of the first item, Clean Up Window, changes. It changes to reflect the last viewing order of that window. For example, if you had the window set to view by date, change the view to icon, and then hold down the OPTION key while clicking on the Special menu; the first item reads Clean Up By Date. We find this most useful when we want to sort items in a window by name.

Be Careful When Renaming or Trashing Files to Make Sure They Aren't Open

When applications are open, their Finder icons become grayed out as a visual indicator that they are open. However, icons of documents are not grayed out when they are open. Since you get no visual indication that a file is open, this means you can inadvertently rename them or even drag them to the trash. However, you cannot usually empty the trash when it contains a file that is open (in use) in an application.

Renaming or trashing a file that an application currently has open can lead to unpredictable results. Some programs deal with this situation more elegantly than others. For example, when you save an open Microsoft Word document that has been renamed or trashed, it presents you with a standard Save dialog box to let you give the file a new name.

The best solution is to make sure that when you are working with files, to close all documents in open applications, or you can just check by bringing applications to the front to make sure the documents you are manipulating are not open.

Two Ways to Bypass the Empty Trash Warning

By default, when you empty the trash, it first presents a dialog box telling you how many items the trash contains, the amount of space they use, and asks if you're sure you want to delete them permanently, as shown here:

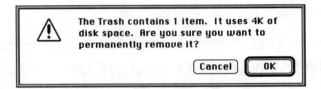

If this dialog irritates you, here's how to turn if off. Uncheck the Trash Get Info box labeled "Warn before emptying" in the Trash Get Info window. To summon this window, select the trash can and use the Finder's Get Info command, as shown here:

This Info window is also useful for telling you how many items are in the trash and how much free space you will get when you empty the trash.

If you like, you can leave the box checked and still bypass the warning dialog on a case-by-case basis by holding down the OPTION key when you empty the trash.

Rescue Items from the Trash with the Put Away Command

TIP 55

You can always drag something out of the Trash if you change your mind about deleting it. However, you'll want a better way if you've dragged several items from different folders to the Trash or if you've closed a deeply nested folder after dragging an item from it to the Trash. The Finder provides a better way, and it's the Finder's File menu Put Away command. Select any items in the Trash you want to retrieve and issue the Put Away command. (You won't be able to use the Put Away command if you've replaced the item in the Trash with an item of the same kind with the same name.)

How to Force the Trash to Empty, Even When It Contains Locked Items

TIP 56

Normally, the Finder will refuse to empty the Trash if it contains any items that are locked, and any folders containing those items. The tedious way to get around this is to open the Trash, find those files and unlock them. The easier way to get around it is to hold down the OPTION key while you choose the Empty Trash command; the Finder will not warn you about the locked items, but instead will empty the Trash without comment.

Selecting More than One Item at a Time

TIP 57

Making selections is one of the most basic features of the Finder. It's both intuitive and very useful. Clicking to select a single item works well, as does the click-and-drag technique to select multiple, contiguous items. The technique to select multiple, noncontiguous items is called SHIFT-clicking and what it lacks in intuitiveness, it more than makes up for in utility. As the name implies, by holding down the SHIFT key you can click to select as many items as you need. The only restriction is that all the items be in the same folder (unless you are using a list view, as discussed in Tip 61).

How to Use the Keyboard to Select and Manipulate Finder Items

You aren't limited to using the mouse in System 7 to select icons in the Finder, you can use the keyboard as well. Here's a table that shows how to select files in Finder windows using the keyboard:

Keystroke:	Action in Icon View
any characters	Selects closest file that matches those characters
TAB	Selects next file alphabetically
SHIFT-TAB	Selects previous file alphabetically
Z-UP ARROW	Opens folder containing current one
Z-DOWN ARROW	Opens selected folder
OPTION-⌘-UP ARROW	Opens folder containing current folder and closes current folder
Z-SHIFT-UP ARROW	Makes desktop active
Arrow keys	Select adjacent icons
RETURN key	Selects text of the icon's name

Any icon can be selected by typing its name. For example, typing an **a** selects the first file that begins with that letter. Typing **a** and **p** in rapid succession selects the first file that begins with ap. If you delay for a short time after typing the a, and then type the p, the first icon beginning with the letter p is selected, and so on.

In List views, the LEFT ARROW and RIGHT ARROW keys have no effect in selecting icons. Instead, they place the insertion at the beginning or ending of the currently selected filename for editing purposes.

The TAB key selects the next icon alphabetically without regard to the current sort order of the window. That is, even if the window is set to view by size, the next icon alphabetically is selected; use UP ARROW or DOWN ARROW keys to select the file above or below the one currently selected.

How to Copy a File to a New Location Instead of Just Moving It

Dragging a file or folder to a different folder moves it. If you want to copy a file or folder (leaving the originals undisturbed), hold down the OPTION key while dragging.

How to Use Finder Outline Views

Finder outline views are very useful for several reasons, listed in Tips 62 and 63. Here's a rundown on how to use them:

Finder outline views are available in any of the list views—that is, when a window is set to be viewed by name, size, kind, label, or date. In any of these views, folder icons have a small triangle to their left, as shown here:

System Folder			
33 items	180.7 MB in disk		20 MB available
Name	Size	Kind	Label
▷ 🗀 Apple Menu Items	333K	folder	—
▷ 🗀 Apple Menu Items (disabl...	158K	folder	—
▷ 🗀 AppleLink Out Basket	14K	folder	—
🗋 CD Remote Programs	7K	CD Remote INIT do...	—
▷ 🗀 Claris	5,485K	folder	—
🗋 Clipboard	4K	file	—
▷ 🗀 Control Panels	2,706K	folder	—
▷ 🗀 Control Panels (disabled)	1,012K	folder	—
🗋 CTB Resources	84K	file	—
▷ 🗀 DataViz	1,768K	folder	—
🗋 Disinfectant Prefs	4K	Disinfectant docum...	—
▷ 🗀 Duplicate Items	46K	folder	—
▷ 🗀 DynoPage Folder	144K	folder	—
▷ 🗀 Extensions	7,130K	folder	—
▷ 🗀 Extensions (disabled)	1,435K	folder	—
▷ 🗀 FaxSpoolf	126K	folder	—
🗋 Finder	371K	file	—
▷ 🗀 Fonts	5,702K	folder	—
🗋 Hosts	4K	Text document	Hot
🗋 Nisus Preferences 3.0	4K	Nisus preferences	—

When the triangle is pointing to the right, the outline of that folder is said to be *collapsed*. Click the triangle to expand any folder to its outline view.

When a folder is expanded, the triangle points downward, as shown here:

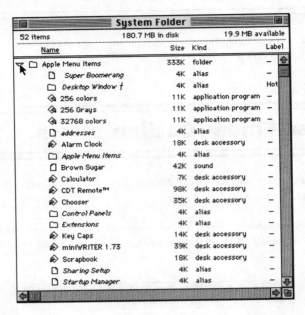

A folder opened as an outline is said to be *expanded*. Note in this example that the outline view of the Apple Menu Items folder has become so long that you can't view all of it without scrolling. Note, too, that there is an icon for an alias of the Desktop Window folder; since this is an alias, it can't be expanded.

You cannot have two views of a folder at the same time: when you open a folder that is currently part of an expanded outline, that expanded outline closes automatically.

Keyboard Shortcuts That Expand and Collapse Icon Views

The Finder has keyboard equivalents for managing outline views:

Keystroke	Action in icon view
Z-RIGHT ARROW	Expands outline of selected folder
Z-LEFT ARROW	Collapses outline of selected folder
Z-OPTION RIGHT ARROW	Expands outline of selected folder *and all the folders it contains*
Z-OPTION LEFT ARROW	Collapses outline of selected folder *and all the folders it contains*

Be careful when using the latter two options. Though they are useful, the Finder slows down considerably when you ask it to change the view of a very large number of folders. For example, expanding the outline of an entire hard disk can take several minutes.

Use Finder Outline Views to Copy Items from Several Folders at Once

TIP 62

Of all the possible views, only Outline views let you gather a number of items from different folders in order to copy them all to a floppy or to a different folder. When folders are displayed as expanded outlines, you can select icons from those different folders by holding down the SHIFT key as you click on the icons.

Use Expanded Outline Views to Print a List of the Contents of a Folder

TIP 63

Outline views are usually the best choice when you want to print the contents of folders, including the contents of all the folders inside folders. To do so, completely expand all the folders (using ⌘-OPTION-RIGHT ARROW to expand a folder). Then use the File menu's Print Window command. But be careful, the Finder can become quite sluggish when you ask it to display a large number of items in a window.

Use OPTION-F (f) to Denote Folder Names

Be careful when giving custom icons to folders to make sure that those icons look like folders. We are also in the habit of appending the word **folder** to names of folders to help us tell that they are not files. Since "folder" might take up too many characters, a good alternative is to use the mathematical function character f at the end of a folder name. You can produce this character by holding down the OPTION key as you press the F key.

How to Create Custom Icons and How They Work

The Finder can create a custom icon out of any graphic you can place on the Clipboard. Assuming you have a graphic on the Clipboard, here's how to give a custom icon to a file, folder, or disk:

1. Select the item you want to change.

2. Use the Get Info command on the File menu.

3. Click on the icon of the item in upper left of the Get Info window to select it. When selected, it looks like this:

```
┌──────────────────────────────────┐
│ ▓▓ ▓  Nightingales Code Info   ▓▓ │
├──────────────────────────────────┤
│  ┌───┐                           │
│  │   │  Nightingales Code        │
│  └───┘                           │
│  Kind : alias                    │
│  Size : 4K on disk (2,574 bytes used) │
│                                  │
│  Where : Mr. Jones : Desktop Window : │
│                                  │
│  Created : Wed, Oct 21, 1992, 3:45 PM │
│  Modified : Wed, May 26, 1993, 10:41 AM │
│  Original : Mr. Jones : Nightingales Code │
│                                  │
│  Comments :                      │
│  ┌────────────────────────────┐  │
│  │                            │  │
│  │                            │  │
│  └────────────────────────────┘  │
│                                  │
│  ☐ Locked      ( Find Original ) │
└──────────────────────────────────┘
```

4. Choose Paste from the Finder Edit menu. If there is no graphic on the clipboard, or if the Finder is somehow unable to convert the graphic to icon size, then the Paste command is grayed and not available.

You can remove any custom icon by pressing the DELETE or BACKSPACE key while the icon is selected in the Get Info window, or by using the Cut or Clear commands on the Edit menu.

Custom icons for files are stored as special resources within the file (their IDs are always -16455, if you must know). Custom icons for folders and disks are stored in invisible files (stored at the top level of the disk or folder to which you have given the custom icon) called, appropriately enough, ICON.

Make Sure Custom Folder Icons Look Like Folders

While custom icons are handy to help you give yourself visual cues as to what a file is all about, we recommend that you assign custom icons to folders with caution. For example, when you give custom icons to folders, try to make sure that either the new icon looks like a folder icon or you use folder or ƒ at the end of the folder's name.

Using Custom Icons Can Slow Opening Folders in Icon Views

As cool as custom icons can be when executed imaginatively, they can exact a price that is paid in performance. Custom icons are stored in the file itself, and are not copied to the desktop file. Thus, each time a window is opened, the Finder must read the icon portion of the file to determine its icon. This can slow opening of folders with many custom icons in them.

Calculate Folder Sizes Slows the Finder Only When the Folder Is Sorted by Size

The Calculate sizes option (which you can turn on using the Views control panel) is very useful. It does take the Finder time to display the size for each folder in a window. However, the process does not slow you down; the Finder calculates folder sizes when it's not otherwise busy. Indeed, you can interrupt the process and open other icons, launch applications, or perform other Finder tasks.

The only time that Calculate folder sizes appreciably slows things down is when you have the folder viewed by size. Since all folder sizes must be calculated before they can be sorted, you can't to do anything else until the Finder has finished calculating all the folder sizes and sorting the items in the window.

If You Have Problems, Delete the Finder Prefs File (and Prefs Files in General) by Moving Them Somewhere Else

As do most applications, the Finder maintains a preferences file inside the Preferences folder in the System Folder. Stored in this file are preferences for all the items the Views control panel lets you change. This file is called Finder Preferences. If the Finder begins to display views improperly (for example, with filenames overlapping), erase the Finder Preferences file (or move it to another location). The Finder automatically re-creates this to its preference file whenever it is absent. Use the Views control panel to re-create your settings easily.

The Finder Rename Delay and How to Avoid It

Time was when all you had to do to edit a filename was to select it and start typing. But apparently this simple technique caused some folks to rename files when they didn't intend to, so System 7 arrived with a rename delay. This delay, which is associated with the double-click setting of the General control panel, is annoying to those sure of what they're doing. Here are three ways to circumvent the rename delay. Choose the one that suits you best:

❏ Click the icon, press the RETURN or the ENTER key, and start typing.

❏ Click on name of the icon and start typing (you don't need to wait for the box to appear around text).

❏ Click on the name of the icon and jiggle the pointer. This technique lets you position the insertion pointer precisely for editing a filename, rather than replacing it.

Keyboard Keys for Editing a Filename

TIP 71

Once you've selected a filename for editing, you can use the keyboard arrow keys to position the insertion pointer. If used immediately after the name is selected, the UP ARROW or LEFT ARROW keys move the insertion pointer to the beginning of the name, while the DOWN ARROW or RIGHT ARROW moves it to the end of the name.

Finder Window Information Isn't Always Up to Date

TIP 72

There are several cases where information you see in a Finder window might not be current. The Finder does not automatically update information contained in open windows on the desktop, but instead updates the information when you open the window.

This means that if you have worked on a document that is located inside an open window and saved that file, the displayed modification date won't be accurate. Normally, this isn't a critical detail. But if the folder is set to be viewed by date, it won't automatically be sorted in the correct order. You can force the update by resorting the folder or by closing it and opening it again.

Related to this is the size of a file shown in a Finder window. If the file that you edited becomes larger or smaller when you save it, the displayed size won't be correct. Again, this really only matters if the window is sorted by size.

To avoid potential problems, it's not a bad idea to get in the habit of closing and opening windows before you rely on information they contain.

How to Hide Windows of Inactive Applications

When you have several applications running, the windows of the applications that are not active (that is, the windows of those applications that are in the background), can at best clutter up the display, and at worst be confusing. You can have the Finder hide the windows associated with all open applications except the active one by pressing the OPTION key when you select an application from the Application menu.

When Clicking on Finder Windows, Clicks Are Passed Through

If you are in an application, and want to switch to the Finder by clicking (rather than choosing Finder from the Applications menu), it's best to click on the desktop behind the current application instead of a Finder window. The reason is that the Finder accepts clicks in any of its windows to select the item you clicked on. By clicking on the desktop, nothing is inadvertently selected, as the Finder simply becomes the active application.

What to Place in the Apple Menu Items Folder

The configurable Apple menu in System 7 is terrific; you can place all kinds of things in it: files, folders, sounds, disk icons, and aliases.

The Apple menu can display only 53 items on the Apple menu; if you put more than 53 items into the Apple Menu Items folder, the excess is ignored.

But we don't recommend that you even approach the 53-item limit. On a 13-inch monitor, about 25 items can be displayed before you have to scroll to the very bottom of the Apple menu to be able to see all of its items. In our experience, the Apple menu is a case of out of sight, out of mind. That is, we forget that we have items on the menu if we can't see them. Further, a large number of items on the Apple menu slows its display, especially scrolling to the bottom items that are not initially displayed. Therefore, we try to never put more than 25 items on the menu.

Limiting the number of items on the Apple menu can best be done if you limit the kinds of items you put on that menu. We put System-related aliases in the menu; that is aliases for tools we use to configure the system, such as the Extensions, Apple Menu Items, and System folders. We also put aliases of other handy folders there, too.

How to Force an Item to the Top of the Apple Menu

TIP 76

Items in the Apple menu are always viewed alphabetically by name. You can force any item to appear at the top of the menu by placing a space at the beginning of its name. To add a space to the name of an item on the menu, open the Apple Menu Items folder in the top level of the System folder. Locate the item you want and add the space to its name.

Use Only Aliases in the Startup Items Folder

TIP 77

Items placed in the Startup Items folder in the System folder are opened automatically by the Finder when the system starts. We recommend that you place only alias files in this folder, not files themselves.

The System folder is for System-related files. Including applications or documents in the Startup Items folder violates the sacrosanct everything-in-its-place rule that helps ensure a manageable file organization. It's also not easy to control the order in which items in this folder are located (in fact, we haven't been able to determine that order). Aliases in this folder are all opened alphabetically, so you can use spaces and filenames (an alias file named need not be the same as the names of the original, so you have almost total control over the load order) to control the order in which items are opened.

Use Startup Items to Display Standard Windows

As mentioned in Tip 44, we use and recommend the technique of maintaining a special folder on the desktop that is used to contain aliases of frequently used items. We place an alias of this folder in the Startup Items folder and change its name so it is opened last. That way, each time the system starts up, this folder always opens to be the frontmost window.

Use an Alias of a Desktop Sound in the Startup Items Folder

Starting the Mac can take longer than a few moments, particularly if you have a large number of control panels and extensions. In the morning, we like to start the machine, and then work on that second cup of coffee and the morning crossword puzzle while the machine is starting. We have a digitized version of the beginning of the Rolling Stones' Brown Sugar as a desktop sound, and place an alias of that in our Startup Items folder. Thus, when the Macintosh has finished sounding, Keith Richard helps wake us up. Though perhaps the opening to Start Me Up would be more appropriate.

Clean Up the Preferences Folder Often

While the files in the Preferences folder in the System Folder are generally fairly small, it's a good idea to keep an eye on its contents. When you remove software, you generally don't check this folder. Periodically, we examine this folder's contents, looking for preferences files that are older than about six months. If we no longer have the applications that created the preference files on our hard disk, we trash them.

Create an Applications Folder and Place Applications in It

Applications installed by the Apple Installer are placed in their own folders at the top level of your hard disk. That's fine, to a point. But having a lot of folders at the top level of the hard disk seems untidy to us.

Instead, we recommend that you create a folder called Applications at the top level of your hard disk, and after installing new applications, move their folders into that folder. Then, create an alias of that new application, and place it in the Desktop Window folder, or other folder in which you store aliases. This means you don't need to wade through a lot of folders to find the items you want, and all applications are stored in one neat place.

Some Good Strategies for Storing Documents

First, documents should be stored *separately* from the applications that created them. It's all too common that, for example, Excel spreadsheets are stored in the Excel folder. That's inefficient and cumbersome. It's better to have a separate data folder, in which you store *all* your documents. That folder should, in turn, contain other folders which contain all the files that relate to a certain project. For example, when writing this book, we stored all related files in a folder called Tips Book *f*. We also put an alias of that folder in the Desktop Window folder for easy access. In turn, within the tips folder, we kept folders for the separate sections of the book.

This approach means that when working on a specific project, all the files you need for that project are readily available: you don't need to navigate to separate folders to find that MacWrite Pro document and the Excel spreadsheet you're including in it.

How to Save a Snapshot of the Screen

The Mac has a built-in feature that gives you a simple way to capture a snapshot of the screen (sometimes called a *screen dump*) to a disk file. Press ⌘-SHIFT-3 to create a file on disk in the PICT format. The first screen dump file is saved on disk with the name Picture 1, the second with the name Picture 2, and so on for as many screen dumps as you capture. You can view the file with TeachText. You can open and edit the file with any application that can read the PICT file format, such as ClarisWorks or Adobe PhotoShop. You can also use any of several commercial and shareware utilities that give you a lot more control over the capture such as the ability to capture just the active window or a selection of the screen that you specify, force a color screen capture to monochrome, and save in another file format. We use Capture from Mainstay and FlashIt by Nobu Toge.

You Can View Screen Dumps with the TeachText Application

TeachText, which is included with every Mac, can open screen dumps created with the ⌘-SHIFT-3 key combination. TeachText can also open any PICT format file, regardless of which application created the file. As with text, you can not edit PICT files with TeachText.

How to Find Documents Created by a Specific Application

You can use the More Choices button on the Find dialog to search for all documents created by a particular application. Here's how:

1. Open a folder containing a document of the kind you want to find, and set its view to one of the list views so you can see the Kind column. Note what is entered there for use with the Find File document.

2. Use the Find command to open the Find dialog.

3. Click the More Choice button to expand the dialog.

4. On the pop-up menu at the left edge of the column, choose Kind.

5. Enter either the entire text of what appeared in the Kind column in the window or a portion of it into the rightmost field in the window.

In the following example we are looking for documents created by Microsoft Word. This search specification finds documents created by Microsoft Word and any other application, such as WordPerfect, whose kind includes "Word." (To find only Microsoft Word documents, we would have to enter **Microsoft Word**.)

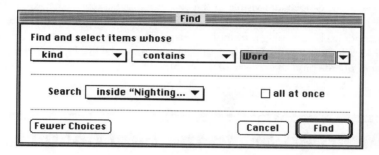

Use the All at Once Check Box in the Find Dialog Judiciously

When you check the All at Once box in the More Choices mode of the Find dialog, the Finder attempts to locate all the files that meet the criteria, and select them at one time. Use this option carefully. If the search process finds too many files, it will fail (how many files it can select depends on how much memory is available to the Finder). It's better to use this option only when you are also restricting searches to a specific folder, as mentioned in Tip 87.

Note, too, that when you check the All at Once box, the box to the left changes to limit the search to only one folder or disk; since there is no outline view of the entire desktop, the Finder cannot display all the files found on a number of volumes at one time.

How to Restrict Finding to a Specific Location with the Find Command

When you have the More Choices view of the Find command dialog visible, a check box and pop-up menu let you limit the locations the Finder searches for files. It always lists all the mounted volumes separately.

However, if a window is open and visible in the background and active (that is, the lines on its title bar are visible), that window will also be listed, and you can restrict the search to that window (and the folders it contains) by choosing it from the pop-up. This is a good way to search, especially if you want to use the All at Once option. Simply locate the topmost folder in which you think the documents might be found, open it, and then use the Find command.

Alternatives to the Find Command

The Finder's Find command is reasonably powerful, but there are several alternatives available from third parties that offer a much wider range of options. The following products fall into this category, and they also can search for text within files: On Technology's On Location, Microlytic's GoFer, Claris' Retrieve It, and Alki's Alki Seek. No Hands Software's Magnet and ZiffNet/Mac's FindPro are also powerful file-searching products that make the Finder Find command seem like a toy in comparison.

About File Types and Creators

This isn't so much a tip as a short lesson in part of how the Finder works. Every Mac file contains information about what kind of file it is, called the *type*, and what application created it, called the *creator*. Each is stored as a four-character label within the file itself.

The type information tells the Finder what kind of file the it is. Many applications can work with more than one type of file, and some file types can be used by a variety of applications. Common file types include TEXT for a file containing only text, and PICT for a graphic. When you open a file from within an application, the application notifies the Finder about what type of documents it can open, and only these document types are shown in the Open file dialog.

The creator information is the four-character signature of the application that created the file. Each application must have its own creator signature, and Apple keeps a registry of them. Developers notify Apple of their creator signature when they make a new application, and Apple notifies them if the signature is already taken. The Finder uses this information to determine which application to use to open a file that you double-click. It looks up the creator information in its desktop files. If that application is available on any mounted volume, the Finder then automatically launches the application which in turn opens the file. If the application is not available, the Finder displays a dialog box stating that the application that created the application that created the file cannot be found.

If you don't have the application that created the file, but you know that you have an application that can open it, the workaround is to drag and drop the icon of the file to the icon of the application that can open it. For example, you can drag and drop a Microsoft Word file onto the ClarisWorks icon.

What Good Is Knowing File Type and Creator Information?

File type and creator information normally is handled transparently for you, and you don't need to worry about it. There are, however, instances in which the information is useful.

First, some communications programs let you assign types and creators to files that are downloaded. These are then handled automatically. Though some of these programs allow you to do this by locating the application, others require that you type the creator codes directly.

Second, most disk recovery programs and unerase utilities (such as Central Points MacTools and the Norton Utilities) display these codes when displaying lists of files to be recovered or undeleted. Knowing the codes helps you determine which files to recover.

Third, if you don't have an application that created a specific file, then you can use these codes to help determine whether another program will open them.

Finally, scripting systems such as AppleScript and UserLand Frontier allow you to examine type and creator codes for files, and perform certain operations based on those codes.

There are several utilities, including ResEdit, that allow you to change the type and creator codes for documents. We also use BunchTyper, which allows us to change the codes of a number of documents at once.

If you get a PICT file from someone, and don't have the application they used to create the PICT file, it will be opened with TeachText when you double-click it. For one or two files, it's useful to drag and drop it onto another application. But if you have a lot of files, you'd rather be able to double-click them. Thus, changing their creators to that of the application you do have, lets you do this. The same is true of TEXT files.

File Types and Creators for Common System Files

The following table lists the types and creators for some common files created by the system itself or by operations you commonly perform with the system.

Note that some items in the table have no entries in the Creator column. That's because they vary between instances of the common type. For example, while the general type for control panels is cdev, the creator of each control panel is unique to that control panel. By the same token, all applications have the type APPL, but their creators vary.

Common File Kind	Type	Creator
The System File	zsys	MACS
Application program		APPL
Control Panel	cdev	
Extension		INIT
Chooser Extension for network access		RDEV
Chooser device for printer		PRER
Desk Accessory	dfil	
Desktop Sound	sfil	
Clipboard	CLIP	MACS
QuickTime component	thng	
Control Panels folder alias	fact	MACS
Extensions Folder alias	faex	MACS
System Folder alias	fasy	MACS
System Resource file	ZSYS	MACS
Folder alias	fdrp	MACS

Common File Kind	Type	Creator
Application alias	adrp	
Communication Toolbox extension	cbnd	ctbc
Desktop DB file	BTFL	DMGR
Desktop DF file	DTFL	DMGR
Desktop (from System 6)	FNDR	ERIK
TeachText read only file	ttro	ttxt
TeachText text file	TEXT	ttxt
HyperCard stack	STAK	WILD
AppleScript Scripting Addition	osax	ascr
Font suitcase	FFIL	DMOV
PostScript font file	LWFN	ASPF
AppleScript dropable application	APPL	dplt
AppleScript application	APPL	aplt
AppleScript compiled script	osas	ToyS
QuickTime Movie		MooV

File Types and Creators for Common Applications

TIP 92

Application	Creator
4th Dimension	4D02
Acta 7_ 1.0.3	ACTA
Acta	ACTA
Adobe Illustrator	ARTY
Adobe Photoshop_ 2.5	8BIM
Aldus Fetch 1.0	Ftch
Aidus Freehand	ACA3
Aldus PageMaker 3.0	ALD3
Aldus PageMaker 4.x	ALD4
Aldus Persuasion	PLP1
Apple DocViewer	HLX2
AppleLink	GEOL
Claris CAD	CCAD
ClarisWorks	BOBO
DATEBOOK_ PRO	DBPR

Application	Creator
DD Expand_	DDAP
Deneba Canvas	DAD2
Disk Copy 4.2	dCpy
Dynodex 3.0	DYNO
Easy View	ezVu
EasyPlay 2.0	EZpa
FileMaker Pro	FMPR
HyperCard	WILD
JPEGView	JVWR
Lotus 1-2-3	L123
MacDraft	MACD
MacroMedia Director	MMDR
MacWrite II	MWII
MacWrite Pro	MWPR
Microsoft Excel	XCEL
Microsoft Word	MSWD
More II	MOR2
Nisus_ 3.06	NISI
Panorama	KAS1
QuarkXPress	XPRS
ResEdit	RSED
ScreenPlay	SPLY
Script Editor	ToyS
Scriptable Text Editor	quil
Simple Player	TVOD
StuffIt Deluxe_ 3.0.5	SIT!
TeachText 7.1	ttxt
TOUCHBASE_ PRO	TBap
WordPerfect	WPC2

Computing with No System Alert Sounds

Most of the time the Mac system alert sounds create very little disturbance. But if for some reason they are annoying your coworkers, or if you're using a PowerBook in bed next to a slumbering mate, you might be asked to pipe down. (In the latter case you might also be asked to make a choice.) If so, mute your Mac by setting the Sound control panel's Speaker Volume slider control to 0. Instead of sounding the alert sound, the Mac flashes the menu bar when the slider is set to 0.

Accessing Remote Volume Desktop Files with Open and Save Dialog Boxes

Using Open and Save file dialogs is relatively straightforward. But we've noticed that users sometimes have trouble finding files that are located on the desktop of remote networked Macs. When you navigate to the desktop, you see only the files on your local Mac's desktop. The files on the desktop of a remote volume are stored in a folder called Desktop Folder that appears in the Open and Save dialogs in the top directory of the remote volume.

Keep Any Folder That You Refer to Frequently Close at Hand

If you find yourself working on several short-term projects simultaneously, try keeping the folders relating to those projects on the desktop. That way, they're easy to access, and they also serve as a constant reminder of what needs your attention. If keeping several folders around on the desktop offends your sense of order, you might prefer to keep all your project folders together in a single folder on the desktop. We sometimes combine this technique with the Desktop Window folder trick described in Tip 44. If we know that we're going to be working on a specific file for some time, we leave its original in its proper folder with the rest of its related file and put an alias of it in the Desktop Window folder. When the project is completed, we enjoy the well-deserved satisfaction of trashing the alias, secure in the knowledge that the original is prudently stored in its folder.

Use the Date in Names of Files That You're Archiving

The Finder does a pretty good job of letting you manage files by date, but there may be occasions when adding the date of the file to the beginning of its name helps you keep them organized. Here are three examples:

1. At the weekly magazine *MacWEEK*, files are organized by the date of the issue. All files for the October 11 issue begin with 1011. So the "Mac the Knife" column for that week's issue is named 1011Knife; a review of this book might be named 1011TipsBookReview. This way, the many editors and production people who put the magazine together each week can spot the files relevant to each week's issue at a glance. When the issue is completed, it's easy to archive all the files beginning with "1011."

2. You're a student and your fiancee is in another country defending the interests of this one. You write to your beloved every day, and of course want to keep a copy of each day's letter for the ages. Name them in the format *MMDDYY*Sweetheart (where *MM* is the number of the month, *DD* is the day and *YY* is the year).

3. The Department of Public Works promised to pave your street two months ago. Each week you write a letter reminding it of that fact. Your attorney can organize your case more efficiently if you use the date in the filename for each week's letter.

When Collaborating on the Same Document, Append Initials to the End of the Filenames

If you're collaborating with others on the same file, you can more easily keep track of the revisions if you attach to the filename the initials of the person who last revised it. For example, each chapter of this book originated as a file that we passed back and forth several times and we used this technique of adding our initials. As the work progressed, the file had the names 1-Finder; 1-Finder,dc; 1-Finder,dc,sm; 1-Finder,dc,sm,dc; and 1-Finder,dc,sm,dc,sm. This way we always knew who had last edited the file and thus to whom to direct recriminations.

A Slick Way to Recover from a Corrupted System File

Sometime, when you least expect it, your System file will become corrupted. The obvious way out of this particular mess is to reinstall from the copies of the System distribution disks. The drawback to this solution is that you then have to reset all of your preferences, plus any sounds or other resources that you've installed in the System in the course of customizing your Mac. This can be very time consuming. We avoid this problem by keeping a StuffIt archive of our System file and Preferences folder. (Other compression products would probably work, but we stick with StuffIt.) If the System file becomes corrupted, all we have to do is delete it and the Preference folder and decompress from the archive.

To Sort Files in Numeric Order, Make Sure You Pad with Zeros, so They Sort Right

Here is a list of filenames that are padded with zeros to sort properly:

        001TEXT
        002TEXT
        003TEXT
        ...
        010TEXT

If you don't pad with the zeros before the number, file 10 will sort before file 2.

How to Deal with the "Do You Want to Initialize This Disk" Dialog

Sometimes when you insert a disk into your Macintosh, you'll get this alert:

> **This is not a Macintosh disk:**
> **Do you want to initialize it?**
>
> [Eject]   [Initialize]

If the disk is a new one, of course you'll want to initialize it so your Mac can use it.

However, sometimes you get this error on a disk that you know contains files. There are several reasons this can happen. First, the disk might have been formatted by a PC, and the formats used by DOS are different than those used by Macs. In this case, consult Part 4 for a list of programs that allow your Mac to read DOS disks.

However, sometimes you get the error with a Mac disk on which you know files are stored. There are a few things to do to handle this:

❑ **Click the Eject button and reinsert it** Sometimes ejecting a disk and reinserting it can cause it to be read; perhaps, when it was inserted the first time, it didn't get seated in the drive in quite the correct way. If the disk has just been moved from an environment of different temperature than normal (such as a briefcase), you can wait a few minutes for the disk's temperature to change and attempt to read it then.

❑ **Try it in another drive** If the disk still cannot be read by your disk drive, try one in a different Mac; this often works with disks that were formatted on different machines. With use, the heads on floppy disk drives sometimes become slightly miscalibrated, sometimes enough to make a disk formatted on one machine unreadable on another.

❑ **Use a utility package** If neither of these approaches works, try a utility such as the Norton Utilities or Central Point's MacTools (we prefer the latter). These programs can recover data from damaged floppy disks and are very useful.

After you have recovered the data from a problematic floppy, throw it away. If you insist on continuing to use a floppy that has been a proven problem maker, initialize it using the Erase Disk command. When the Finder erases a disk, it verifies the entire disk and rejects it if it has serious problems. If the Finder rejects the disk, its useful life is over.

Don't Force a Disk Out of a Drive

If a disk becomes stuck in a drive, *do not* attempt to force the disk out! If a disk is forcibly ejected from a drive, the drive can become severely damaged (we've been there—we know). Check the Macintosh's case around the drive to make sure there's room for it to be ejected (sometimes cases don't get put back together correctly after they've been taken apart). Push the disk back in to get it seated, then attempt to eject it again. Often disks eject successfully on the second attempt.

If worst comes to worst, and you can't get the floppy out, take the Mac apart and try to remove the disk gently; if you aren't comfortable doing that, take the Mac to a service location. It's better to spend $50 or $75 for the help of a service person to eject a disk than it is to spend more than $200 for repairs to a floppy drive! Also, the service person might discover and repair the root cause of the disk not ejecting.

Copying the Date and Time from the Alarm Clock Desk Accessory

You can copy the date and time from the Alarm Clock desk accessory. Make it the frontmost window (click on it to make sure), and use the Copy command on the Edit menu (⌘-C, of course). This places the date and time on the Clipboard, with the time first, followed by a space, and then the date. The format of the time and date placed on the Clipboard is governed by settings specified in the Date and Time control panel.

Copying and Pasting with the Calculator Desk Accessory

You can copy numbers and symbols into the Calculator desk accessory, and it accepts them just as if you had typed them directly. It accepts numbers and symbols in the same sequence that you had typed them. For example, if you type the text 3*5 into your word processor, select it and copy it, open the Calculator desk accessory and paste—you'll see the keys light up as if you had typed them on the numeric keypad. The text you paste cannot contain any characters other than numbers and the symbols +,–,=,/, and *. If you attempt to paste any other characters (including the space) into the calculator, it will beep and not accept any more characters.

Results shown in the Calculator's display can be copied (though they can't be selected). With the Calculator in front, use the Copy command to place values shown in its window onto the Clipboard.

PART 2

Other System Software

One of the benefits of System 7.1 is its modular nature; Apple can more easily expand its capabilities and adapt it to new Mac models by adding new extensions and control panels. Previously, every new Mac arrived with an upgrade to the system software. In this part, we give you some tips and answer some questions about five key technologies you can add on to System 7.1.

The Easy Access Control Panel Is for Everyone

Usually considered only as an aid for the physically impaired, Easy Access is a control panel that is installed automatically when you install System 7 (any version). It lets you control the Mac without using the mouse, and to use command-key combinations (such as ⌘-O) without having to press both keys simultaneously.

Sometimes these two features can be more useful than you might first think. We have found Easy Access useful for those rare occasions when the mouse stopped working, but when the keyboard still works. It's also useful for other purposes, as we'll mention in Tip 105.

How to Use Easy Access Mouse Keys

Mouse Keys is the Easy Access feature that lets you drive the mouse pointer by using the numeric keypad instead of (or in addition to) the mouse. To enable Mouse Keys, check the On box of the Mouse Keys portion of the Easy Access Control Panel, as shown on the following page.

```
┌─────────────────────────────────────────┐
│ ▦▦▦▦▦▦═══ Easy Access ═══▦▦▦▦▦▦          │
├─────────────────────────────────────────┤
│ ☒ Use On/Off audio feedback             │
│ ┈┈┈┈┈┈┈┈┈┈┈┈┈┈┈┈┈┈┈┈┈┈┈┈┈┈┈┈┈┈┈┈┈       │
│ Mouse Keys:      ◉ On   ○ Off           │
│    Initial Delay :  ○○◉○○               │
│                    long    short         │
│    Maximum Speed :  ○○  ◉○○○    ○○       │
│                    slow  medium   fast   │
│ ┈┈┈┈┈┈┈┈┈┈┈┈┈┈┈┈┈┈┈┈┈┈┈┈┈┈┈┈┈┈┈┈┈       │
│ Slow Keys:       ○ On   ◉ Off           │
│    Acceptance Delay :  ○○◉○○             │
│                       long   short       │
│ ☒ Use key click sound                   │
│ ┈┈┈┈┈┈┈┈┈┈┈┈┈┈┈┈┈┈┈┈┈┈┈┈┈┈┈┈┈┈┈┈┈       │
│ Sticky Keys:     ○ On   ◉ Off           │
│ ☒ Beep when modifier key is set         │
└─────────────────────────────────────────┘
```

With this box checked, activate Mouse Keys by pressing ⌘-SHIFT-CLEAR simultaneously (the CLEAR key is on the numeric keypad). You'll hear a short tone of rising pitch that signifies that Mouse Keys has been enabled. You can then drive the mouse using the numeric keypad. To disable Mouse Keys, press the CLEAR key. A short tone of falling pitch signifies that Mouse Keys has been turned off.

In addition to letting you use the keypad to simulate mouse movements, Mouse Keys provides keys on the keypad that let you duplicate pressing the mouse button. Both the 5 and . keys on the numeric keypad simulate clicking the mouse button. Tap either of them quickly for a double-click. The 0 key on the keypad locks down the mouse button for dragging.

Mouse Keys is especially useful in desktop publishing or graphics programs when you need to nudge a selection in very small increments.

How to Use Easy Access Slow Keys

TIP 106

Easy Access Slow Keys is a very irritating feature unless you have a physical impairment, in which case you might find it indispensible. Slow Keys makes your keyboard feel as if it's operating in slow motion. When this feature is enabled (which you do by holding the RETURN key down for about eight seconds), you need to hold down any key for several seconds before it is actually accepted by the Macintosh (that is, entered into the selection). You can change this delay by changing which radio button in the Control Panel is selected.

TIP 107 — How to Use Easy Access Sticky Keys

Normally, to enter commands from the keyboard, you need to press several keys at the same time, such as the ⌘-O combination to open a document. Sticky Keys lets you press these keys in sequence, and gives you feedback at the upper-right corner of the menu bar as to which key has been pressed.

To enable Sticky Keys, press the SHIFT key five times, without moving the mouse between presses. When Sticky Keys is activated, you hear a short rising tone, and this symbol appears at the top of the menu bar, telling you that Sticky Keys is enabled:

After that, when you press a modifier key (without simultaneously pressing another key) such as the OPTION, SHIFT, or ⌘ keys, the symbol on the right of the menu bar changes to this:

This means that the next keystroke you type will have the modifier key applied to it, after which the modifier is nullified (no longer in effect).

You can "lock" the modifier key by depressing it twice, and the menu bar changes to look like this:

This means that the modifier key will be applied to all keystrokes typed until you press another modifier key.

To turn Sticky Keys off, press the SHIFT key five times in a row again, or simultaneously press any two modifier keys.

What's QuickTime? or The Magic of Moving Pictures

QuickTime is a System extension that allows the Mac to record, compress, and play videos called movies, and provides a standard file format for containing those movies. The movies can be created with many standard Macintosh animation programs or captured from sources such as video tape or laser disc. Movies can contain several tracks for different types of data, such as video and audio. In fact, movies can be created that contain only audio.

QuickTime also provides routines utilizing the JPEG compressing technique that can compress still images as well.

How and Where to Acquire QuickTime

The QuickTime extension is included with Mac system software 7.1, whether you get the complete package or the update version. Upgrades to QuickTime (such as to version 1.6, mentioned in Tip 110) are available from user groups and online services.

In addition to the QuickTime extension, you need an application to play movies. Many general productivity programs, as diverse as Microsoft Word 5.1 and Claris FileMaker Pro 2.0 and ClarisWorks 2.0, can play movies. Other programs, some of which are mentioned in Tip 116, are dedicated to creating or playing movies.

Apple sells a package called the QuickTime Starter Kit (available by mail order for less than $150) that includes utilities for capturing and editing movies and converting other types of animations to movies. It also includes a CD-ROM with lots of QuickTime movies.

What QuickTime 1.6 Can Do for You

In May 1993, Apple released the latest version of QuickTime, 1.6. This version has some advantages over previous versions:

It uses less memory. When the QuickTime extension is loaded, but no movies are playing, it uses 20 to 36Kb of RAM, a substantial improvement over the 160Kb version 1.5 uses. No matter, the savings is still substantial over the 160Kb of RAM used by QuickTime 1.5.

When a movie is actually playing, QuickTime grabs another approximately 500Kb of RAM in the System Heap; the exact amount varies according to the size of the movie being played. When the movie has stopped playing and is closed, QuickTime frees most of that extra memory.

Performance increases. QuickTime 1.6 plays movies about ten percent faster than version 1.0 or 1.5 did. Every ounce of performance improvement you can squeeze out of QuickTime makes movies play back more smoothly and realistically.

QuickTime 1.6 allows you to convert audio tracks on CD audio disks to QuickTime movies on your hard disk, if you are using a CD-ROM drive that supports this feature.

QuickTime 1.6 is available from several sources. If you do not have QuickTime, purchase the QuickTime Starter Kit from your dealer; be sure to get the 1.6 or later version. QuickTime is also one of the rare Apple System Software offerings that is available via online sources and user groups. Dealers should also let you copy it to a floppy.

What You Need to Create a QuickTime Movie

To create a movie, you need software and/or hardware that supports QuickTime movie generation. If you are digitizing movies from a video source, you need a method of connecting your Mac to the video source. At press time, the leading board for this task is SuperMac's VideoSpigot. The VideoSpigot is available for many different Mac models, including the LC series and NuBus-equipped Macs. Other boards are also available, and new ones are coming to market, so check the trade magazines and possibly your dealer to see what's the latest available.

You can create sound-only QuickTime movies in several ways. As mentioned in the next tip, if you have a Macintosh with a built-in microphone, you can create QuickTime movies very easily. You can also use products such as MacroMedia's MacRecorder to create sound movies.

Many animation packages for the Mac (of the kind that let you draw animations on the screen such as Promotion by Motion Works International Inc.) also let you save their results as QuickTime movies.

Free Up as Much Memory as You Can before Recording a QuickTime Movie

TIP 112

When recording QuickTime movies, you need all the memory you can get; QuickTime movies record much faster to memory than to disk, so the best strategy is to give your recording application as much memory as you can. Turn off all extensions and control panels that you don't absolutely need while recording. This has two advantages: Extensions and control panels not only occupy RAM, they often consume processing cycles your recording application might need.

After taking these steps, use the Finder's About this Macintosh command to see how much memory is available and then use the Finder's Get Info command to set the Preferred Memory Size of the recording application as large as possible.

Defragmenting Your Hard Disk Can Improve QuickTime Movie Recording Performance

TIP 113

Even if you assign as much memory as possible to the recording application, it still needs to write to disk. When recording movies, every last bit of performance counts. The time it takes the heads on your hard disk to move from place to place on a fragmented disk can mean lost frames from a movie. So if your hard disk's fragmented, defragment it before recording. This is especially important when recording long movies. You can defragment your hard disk either by backing it up, reformatting and restoring it, or by backing it up and then using a commercial defragmentation utility such as Central Point's MacTools or the Norton Utilities from Symantec Corp.

Record QuickTime Movies with 24-Bit Video

When QuickTime movies are being played back, they look fairly good on systems displaying less than thousands or millions of colors. However, it's best to record movies with the Monitors control panel set to millions of colors (24-bit video). Otherwise, *posterizing* occurs (posterizing happens when software reduces the number of colors in an original to fewer colors) resulting in less satisfactory movie quality.

Use a Clean Source for QuickTime Movies

Since a digitized version of a movie is never better than the original source, use the best quality original that you can. For example, a laserdisc is a better source than a video tape, and an original video tape yields better results than a copy of a video tape.

Low-Cost QuickTime Player Solutions

In order to *play* QuickTime movies, you need application software. Fortunately, many popular commercial applications allow you to insert movies into their documents. Among these are Microsoft Word 5.1, Claris FileMaker Pro 2.0, and ClarisWorks 2.0. But there are also several low-cost, shareware or public domain movie players available. Here's a rundown of several of them:

❑ *Simple Player* is included with Apple's QuickTime Starter kit. It's a good, basic utility. Though it cannot capture movies from video sources on its own, it will allow you to create new movies, and put data into them by cutting and pasting. It can also convert movies from one compression standard to another (see Tip 122).

❑ *Popcorn* is a useful player written by the talented and prolific Leonard Rosenthol of Aladdin Systems. Popcorn was written for the Berkeley Macintosh User Group (BMUG), which wanted to include a player in the TV-ROM, its first CD-ROM of QuickTime movies. Apple would not license BMUG rights to Simple Player, so Rosenthol stepped into the breach with Popcorn. Popcorn is a no-frills player; it doesn't save movies or let you create new ones, but it is useful for playback.

❑ *MovieMaker* is a shareware program that allows you to turn entire folders full of PICT images into QuickTime movies. Make sure that all the PICT images are the same size.

❑ *EasyPlay* is by Michael O'Connor, author of the nearly essential CompuServe Navigator program. In addition to playing QuickTime movies, EasyPlay can create catalogs of movies, featuring thumbnail images from the movies. EasyPlay is Shareware.

❑ *PICTShow* displays slide shows of either QuickTime movies or of PICT files. This nifty application by Oliver Dreer is Freeware.

❑ *MovieConverter* does a couple of handy things. It can create new movies or convert existing animations (such as PICT animations or folders full of PICT files) into QuickTime movies. It can also open existing movies and save them to different formats, allowing you to translate them between compressors.

How to Copy CD Audio Tracks to Your Hard Disk

QuickTime 1.6 lets you copy audio tracks from an audio disc in your CD-ROM drive to your hard disk. You must use an Apple CD 300 model CD-ROM drive to use this feature. (It contains a capability called sound through SCSI that not all other drives have.)

Within any application that can open QuickTime movies, all you have to do is select a file on the CD audio disks (the tracks are named numerically beginning with Track 1). This summons a dialog box that asks where you want to save the QuickTime version of the sound. Choose a volume for saving that has plenty of free space for these corpulent QuickTime movie files.

How to Make a QuickTime Movie a Part of the Startup Sequence

You can instruct your Mac to play a QuickTime movie at startup. Place the QuickTime movie file in the System Folder (at the top level of the System folder; *not* enclosed in any other folders) and name it Startup Movie. The movie will play immediately after QuickTime loads during the startup process. (An alias of a movie file works just as well as a movie file itself.) But is this really progress? Most of us think the Mac already takes long enough to startup without taking time-out for a movie break.

Keyboard Shortcuts You Can Use When Playing Movies

Here are some handy keyboard equivalents you can use to control the playback of QuickTime movies. Note that not all these keyboard shortcuts work in all environments where you play QuickTime movies. They do work with all the stand-alone QuickTime players we have tested, but often do not work when playing movies within applications—for example, Microsoft Word 5.1 interprets the keystrokes as being sent to the text in the document, not to the QuickTime window.

Keystroke	Action
RIGHT ARROW	Step to next frame.
LEFT ARROW	Step to previous frame.
⌘-LEFT ARROW	Play from current frame reverse.
⌘-RIGHT ARROW	Play from current frame forward.
OPTION-LEFT ARROW	Jump to beginning of movie (or if there is a selection and current frame is within the selection, to the beginning of the selection. If the current frame is after the selection, jump to first nonselected frame.)
OPTION-RIGHT ARROW	Jump to end of movie or selection.
SPACEBAR	Start/Stop playback.
SHIFT	Select/deselect frames when using other techniques to display different portions of the movie.

How to Convert a System File Sound to Desktop Sound

You can easily convert Sound control panel-compatible sounds to small desktop files that play when you open them. To convert a sound to a "desktop" sound, double-click on the System file suitcase containing the sound icons and drag the sound from the suitcase to another location (OPTION-drag it if you want to leave the original sound in the System Folder). The sound dragged from the System suitcase has its own icon that looks like this:

Double-click one of these sound icons to play it.

How to Convert a Desktop Sound File to a QuickTime Movie File

You can convert a desktop sound to a QuickTime movie with almost any program that can play movies. Use the command that lets you open a QuickTime Movie (such as Insert Movie in Word 5.1) and locate a desktop sound file. When you click the Open button, a Save File dialog appears asking you for a name and a location of the new QuickTime movie. When saved, the desktop sound is converted to a QuickTime movie.

QuickTime movies that contain sound only look like regular movies minus the viewing area when they are being played:

You can use the slider to control which part of the sound is played, just as with movies.

When the sound movie is opened, you can play only a part of it using the same techniques you use to view only a part of a QuickTime video movie. You can also edit sounds and save them as different QuickTime movies using the techniques for editing video movies with QuickTime players.

Selecting the Appropriate QuickTime Compressor

QuickTime contains these different kinds of compressors, which are available as options when you save a movie with a utility such as Simple Player. Note that for each of these compression mechanisms, there is a Quality slider that appears in the compression dialog. Using this slider, you can adjust the quality of the compressed movie (and thus its eventual size; greater compression equals lower quality).

Animation

Use this compressor for animation that was *created* on the Mac, rather than imported from another source (such as video), and when the differences between colors in parts of the image are dramatic. It uses a standard technique called Run-Length Encoding (RLE) wherein a number is stored to indicate the number of a color, followed by a number for the number of pixels that contain that color. This explains why "real" video does not compress well with this compressor: few rows of pixels contain all the same color.

Graphics

Use this to compress images stored in 8-bit color (256 colors). This compressor is slow, and does not work well for movies but can be useful for still pictures that you want to save in smaller, more manageable files.

This means that the image quality will probably be better than in other compression schemes, but at the cost of considerably more disk space.

Photo-JPEG

Use this efficient compressor for still images. Since the JPEG standard, called Photo-JPEG in QuickTime application dialog boxes, was designed for still images, it is not suitable for moving images. This format is supported nearly transparently by Mac applications.

Video

This compressor is the one to use if you have digitized video using more than 256 colors. The compressor is designed to be fast at both compressing and decompressing images.

Compact Video

This compressor, first introduced with QuickTime 1.5, compresses to the smallest file size. However, it takes a *very* long time for movies to be compressed with this compressor, though they decompress quickly. If you have an especially long movie, use this compressor as the last step after you've finished all the editing and want to store it in as little space as possible.

The Ins and Outs of Lossy

QuickTime uses a compression method that QuickTime uses for both movies and still images. The compression that QuickTime uses—both for still images and for movies—is called "lossy" compression. When an image is compressed, some of the information in the image is *lost*. So, when testing an compressed image, save the compressed version separately from the noncompressed version to see if the lost information is critical to you; you don't want to discard too much, after all. Another implication of this is that you should avoid repeated compressions of the image. The short version of this advice is to compress a movie only when you are finished with any editing.

Cheap Editing with Simple QuickTime Players

It's not absolutely necessary to purchase an expensive QuickTime movie editing application in order to have some rudimentary editing capabilities (though those expensive programs do give you a lot of bang for your buck). Apple's basic Simple Player lets you copy and paste frames or portions of movies from one movie to another. Use the SHIFT-clicking technique (hold down the SHIFT key while selecting with the mouse) to select frames or portions of movies. You can use the Clear or Cut command to delete portions of movies and the Copy command to save a portion to the Clipboard.

Simple Player lets you create a new movie, so it's easy to paste into the new movie portions you have copied from others. Some other basic QuickTime players, such as Popcorn (Freeware from Aladdin Systems) or Easy Play (Shareware from Mike O'Connor) do not allow you to create *new* movies from within them. However, you can duplicate an existing movie in the Finder and use Clipboard editing techniques to merge movies together.

When to Use QuickTime to Compress PICT Files

TIP 125

QuickTime is useful for more than just displaying moving images. It can also facilitate storage of larger still images. It includes as one of its "components" a compressor for the industry-standard JPEG format. Thus, most applications that let you save PICT images can also compress these images using JPEG. This option is only available if you have QuickTime installed. When these images are saved, they are still seen as PICT files by other applications, which can still open them. Note that if the compressed file is to be opened with an application on another Mac, QuickTime must also be installed on that Mac to view the image.

The efficiency of the compression depends both on the degree of complexity of the image, over which you have no control, and the quality of the saved image, which you control with a slider control.

With QuickTime and the proper utility, you can also read JPEG files created on other platforms. JPEGView and GIFConverter are two shareware programs that can do this, in addition to the otherwise lame TeachText.

What's AppleScript?

TIP 126

AppleScript is Apple's newest Mac technology, and may be confusing to some. While it would take an entire book to explain it fully, here's a brief explanation. AppleScript gives users a new way to control their Macs. For the most part, the Mac is a user-driven machine. For example, you tell the Mac to do such things as open an application or document, select some text and make it bold, and the like, using the mouse and the keyboard. AppleScript gives you another method of doing this through text-based instructions called *scripts*. These scripts allow you to perform virtually the same actions and describe those actions with a series of text commands.

All this may sound suspiciously like the batch files of command-line systems such as DOS, but there are several differences. First, AppleScript is very different than DOS batch files. DOS batch files can manipulate files and launch programs, but they can not communicate with those programs *once they are running*, AppleScript can. For example, a script could tell your word processor to gather all paragraphs that begin with the word "caption" and place them at the end of a document. Scripts can be written to perform common tasks such as backing up recently changed files to a server, of compressing or decompressing files in specific folders. AppleScript can also work over networks, so scripts running on one machine can send instructions to other Macs.

At press time, AppleScript is of limited use because most popular applications aren't "AppleScript-savvy"; they do not include the necessary programming code that lets them understand AppleScript commands. This should change over the next year as developers release upgrades providing full AppleScript support to their major applications.

An Alternative to AppleScript: UserLand's Frontier

TIP 127

In addition to AppleScript, there are other Mac scripting environments on the Macintosh. Chief among these is UserLand's Frontier. Frontier has a very different syntax from AppleScript, but otherwise supports everything AppleScript does, and much more. Since Frontier complies with Apple's "Open Scripting Architecture" it works in tandem with AppleScript; indeed Frontier can edit and run scripts written in AppleScript, and Apple's Script Editor can edit and run scripts written in Frontier's language, provided that you also have Frontier installed on your Mac.

Frontier has several advantages over AppleScript. First, it offers a much wider variety of commands for dealing with files; among its many features, it can copy files, move them to different disks, and read their contents. It even features a utility called Finder Menu that adds a scripting menu to the Finder's menu bar so that you can access your scripts easily.

How to Acquire AppleScript

AppleScript consists of two extensions and a script editor. It is available from the Apple Programmer's and Developer's Association (APDA). A package designed for developers—and including sample code that tells how to make applications AppleScript-savvy—costs about $200. A package for those who want to write or run scripts was not shipping at press time, but will be available for about $20 when it ships sometime this fall. APDA can be reached at (800) 282-2732. This user package is very basic; in addition to AppleScript and the documentation, it also includes a scriptable text editor, but few other utilities. Later in 1993, APDA will release a package with more features for users for less than $50. Finally, there's a version for developers who want to license AppleScript for inclusion with their products.

What Are the Two Kinds of Script Applications

You can save and distribute AppleScript scripts as stand-alone applications. This means that the person using the script does not need to know how to use the Script Editor in order to run the scripts. Here are the two kinds of icons:

Drop Something On Me

Double-Click Me

The first kind of application is just that: an application. It contains a script that runs when you open the application. Its icon is labeled "Double-Click Me" in the illustration. When these applications are created, it can be specified whether the application should display a *splash screen* that you have to dismiss before the script runs or not. (A splash screen is the window that is displayed when you use the Apple menu About this application command.) You can also specify whether the application quits or stays open after the script has run. An example of a script that should be saved as an application is listed in Tip 132.

The second type of application is known as a *grinder* or *droplet*. To activate it, you drop some files on its icon, just as you drop files onto an application to open them. You can drag and drop files, folders, or entire disks onto a grinder. When the application runs, it receives a list of the items dropped on it, and the script specifies what to do with each file.

Two Ways to Tell If an Application Is AppleScript-Savvy

Not all applications are yet "AppleScript-savvy," which means that not all of them can be scripted by AppleScript. An application is AppleScript-savvy if it supports a specific set of Apple events (that let it receive messages from other applications and scripts) and if it contains a special resource, called an *AETE resource*. This resource tells AppleScript which objects and commands the application supports. Assuming you have the Script Editor application, there are two ways you can tell if an application is AppleScript-savvy and determine which objects and commands it supports.

In the Finder, drop the icon of an application onto the Script Editor application; Script Editor will launch and if the application is scriptable, its dictionary (a set of object commands that an application understands) will be opened.

The second way is to choose the File menu's Open Dictionary command from within the Script Editor. This command summons a standard File Open dialog box. Only those applications that support AppleScript (only those with AETE resources) are shown in this dialog box. Double-click on any application that appears to see its dictionary.

Understanding Objects and AppleScript Scripting

AppleScript uses something called the *object model* to facilitate its scripting. Briefly put, the object model is a standard means of dealing with the data that programs use. Different kinds of programs deal with different kinds of data—for example, a word processor knows how to deal with words, lines, pages, sentences, and the like, while a database program knows how to deal with fields and records. The kinds of data different programs deal with are grouped together in *suites* or groups, such as the database suite and the required suite. Added to the set of objects a program supports is a set of *commands*

that act upon those objects. Generally, there are many different kinds of objects, but few commands. Commands let scripts get the values of objects and change them.

All scriptable applications support the required suite—a set of commands that tell applications to open, print, or close documents and to quit.

Other suites include a database suite (also called the table suite because operations on tables are very similar to operations on databases), a word processing suite, a communications suite, and a personal information suite, with more to come.

When you open an application dictionary with the Script Editor, objects and commands that apply to the various suites an application supports are grouped together.

TIP 132 — A Sample Script: Startup

The script shown in this section implements a "start the day" script, one that runs only the first time the Mac is started each day. You can use this simple script as a model to create a more sophisticated script to handle such daily chores as mounting network volumes, copying the most current versions of specific files to your local hard drive, checking e-mail, or almost any other routine task.

To create the script, type its text into the Script Editor, and save the script as an application. Use the pop-up menu labeled Kind to save the script as an application.

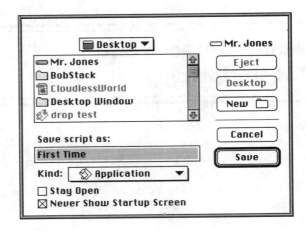

Make sure you check the Never Show Startup Screen box. You can save the application in any folder, but make sure you place an alias of it in the Startup Items folder.

The first line of the script is a property declaration. This property, called "lastTimeIRan" holds the date on which the script last executed. Properties in scripts saved as applications are *persistent* between runs of the application. That is, values in properties are saved to disk (as part of the script) whenever the application quits. This is a handy feature that's also easy to implement. Note that the property is cleared whenever you edit the script and recompile it. In this case, it gives you an easy way to store the date on which the script runs.

The next statement is a test to see if that variable contains anything. The property is empty the first time the script runs after it is compiled, or whenever the script is edited. If the lastTimeIRan property doesn't contain anything, the script copies the current date to the property and runs the runToday handler. Note that the current date is supplied by a Scripting Addition file (found in the Scripting Additions folder inside the Extensions folder). Scripting Additions, like HyperCard XCMDs, become part of AppleScript and are used transparently.

Next in the script is a test to see if the date contained in the lastTimeIRan property is the current date. Since AppleScript doesn't include facilities for operating on dates directly (such as adding or subtracting a year, month, day, or hour), the script stores the current date in a variable called newDate. Note that it must *coerce* the current date from AppleScript's internal date format to text format. Coercion is frequently necessary to convert values from one form to another. When you do this, the date is in the form "Day, Month Date, Year Time AM/PM" so that the current date for the day this is being written is "Thursday, May 6, 1993 6:53:54 PM". The date stored in the variable lastTimeIRan is also coerced to text and stored in a variable called oldDate.

The script then compares the third word of the newDate variable (which contains the day of the month) with the third word of the oldDate variable. If they're different, then the assumption is that the script hasn't been run yet today. Today's date is stored in the persistent lastTimeIRan variable, and the runToday handler is called. Otherwise, since there are no more statements within the main body of the script, the application exits.

So, the upshot of this is that only statements in the runToday handler are called the first time the script runs on any given day.

On successive restarts of the Mac during the day, the script takes only a couple of seconds to run, so it doesn't interrupt you any more than the bomb that probably caused you to restart the Mac in the first place.

```
property lastTimeIRan : ""

if lastTimeIRan is "" then
    copy (current date) to lastTimeIRan
    runToday()
else
    copy (current date) as text to newDate
    copy lastTimeIRan as text to oldDate
    if word 3 of newDate is not word 3 of oldDate then
        copy (current date) to lastTimeIRan
        runToday()
    end if
end if


on runToday()
    -- items placed in this handler run only the first time a
        script runs
    -- on any given day.
end runToday
```

TIP 133

A Sample Script: Folder Watcher

This script gives the skeleton for a grinder, an application on to which you can drop files. It doesn't actually *do* anything with those files; it simply maintains in one of its properties a list of all the files dropped on it. Other scripts, running in the script editor or in other applications can get or clear this list using the getFiles and clearList handlers, as mentioned later.

```
property listOFiles : {} -- the files that have been dropped,
                            stay persistent
on open (theFile)
    copy listOFiles & theFile to listOFiles
    -- just show a dialog telling which files had been dropped
    display dialog (theFile as string)
end open

-- this handler returns a list of all the files that have been
    dropped
-- on this application.
```

```
on getFiles()
    return listOFiles
end getFiles


on clearList() -- purge the listOFiles
    copy {} to listOFiles
end clearList
```

To create this script, type it into the script editor, and save it, as shown here:

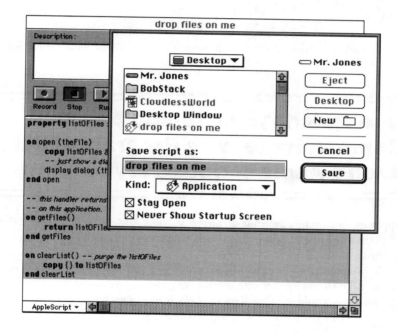

This script is saved as an application. But because the script contains a "handler" for the Open Apple event, the icon of the application changes to include the small arrow pointing into the icon in the Save As dialog box. The Script Editor notes the Open handler and changes the icon for you.

We tell the script to stay open once it has run; this will let other scripts send messages to it.

This script is fairly simple. As with the script in Tip 132, the first line is a property declaration; data stored in this property is saved, even when the script application quits. The handler for the Open event gets a list containing the paths to all the files dropped on the application. In this case, the script saves that list to the listOFiles property and displays a dialog box telling you the name of the file dropped.

Note the presence of two other handlers: one called GetList and one called ClearList. The GetList handler simply returns to the script that called it a list of all the files that have been dropped on it. Here's a short script showing you how to use it:

```
tell application "drop files on me"
    getFiles()
end tell
```

You can use the ClearList handler in the same manner, should you need to purge the list of files.

Use QuicKeys or Tempo to Communicate with Programs That Aren't AppleScript-Savvy

Since most applications currently available do not yet support AppleScript or Frontier, there is a need for a "bridge" to those other applications from a scripting system. Fortunately, two very useful utilities are available that do this: CE Software's QuicKeys and Affinity's Tempo. Both of these utilities can record actions in programs and play them back exactly as if you were doing them yourself. Both of these programs can also receive messages from AppleScript telling them to play their macros. As a short example, here's how you would tell QuicKeys to play a macro from AppleScript:

```
tell app "CEIAC"
    playbyname "myMacro"
end tell
```

The CEIAC application is installed as part of the QuicKeys application automatically, and starts when your Macintosh starts; it must be running in order for QuicKeys to be controlled by AppleScript.

WorldScript Helps Applications to Be Multilingual

WorldScript is part of System 7.1 that makes the operating system more amenable to use with other languages, particularly non-Roman languages. It includes within it support for those languages that need two bytes to store their character information (such as Japanese and Chinese), and allows Mac text editors to work better with language systems that are not read or entered left to right. WorldScript allows Apple to develop extensions to support those languages more effectively, and makes it easier for developers to add support for them to their own products. WorldScript also allows for mixing of language systems within documents; a word processing document could include text in Japanese, Chinese, and English, for example, if it supports WorldScript.

WorldScript by itself can not be purchased directly. Instead, separate language kits must be purchased. At press time, the only one shipping is the Japanese language kit. This kit is available for about $249. It largely replaces Apple's earlier effort, called KangiTalk, for supporting Japanese.

Two Mac word processors currently support WorldScript: WordPerfect Corp.'s WordPerfect 2.1 and Nisus Software Inc.'s Nisus 3.4.

What Is Macintosh Easy Open?

Macintosh Easy Open is a combination of a control panel and extension that makes it easier to work with documents created with applications not available on your Mac and documents created by applications on other computer platforms, such as DOS or Windows.

When you install the software and restart, it first rebuilds the desktop of each volume as it mounts. It records not only the names and native types of all your applications, but also keeps a list of all the different types of documents these applications can open. Thereafter, when you attempt to open a document for which you do not have the creating application, Macintosh Easy Open presents a list of the applications that can open that document, and asks which one you want to launch. If a translator is necessary to open the document, it shows that the translator will be used. The document is then translated (if necessary), the application launched, and the document opened.

Macintosh Easy Open is one of the most useful Macintosh system extensions we have used. We recommend it (and the DataViz translators that currently support it) highly; even if you do not regularly use documents created on other computers, it is handy when you need it.

How to Acquire Macintosh Easy Open

Macintosh Easy Open is not available as a product from Apple, nor indeed from other developers. Instead, it is available as part of other software. At press time it is only available as part of verions 7.02 of DataViz' MacLink Plus/PC.

Turn off the Macintosh Easy Open "Always Show Choices" Preference in the Control Panel

The Macintosh Easy Open Control Panel, shown here, includes a check box labeled Always Show Choices. When this box is checked, Macintosh Easy Open always lists all relevant translators when opening documents not native to your application. This can be very irritating if, for example, you simply want to insert a PICT graphics file in a Microsoft Word document; since Word can read PICT files directly even though PICT files are not stored in the Word format, a list of available translators is superfluous. In this case, turn the Always Show Choices preference off.

Macintosh Easy Open Setup
Macintosh Easy Open v.1.0   ⦿ On © Apple Computer, Inc. 1992   ○ Off
☐ Always Show Choices ☐ Include Choices from Servers
[Delete Preferences...]

What Will Apple Open Collaboration Environment (AOCE) Do for You?

Apple Open Collaboration Environment (AOCE) is an as-yet-unreleased set of system extensions that provides for the integration of electronic mail, voice mail, fax, general telephone support, and other services into the Macintosh. It will provide a standard system platform that developers can use to add mail services and directory services (lists of all users to and from whom you normally receive mail) to their applications. Mailing a document to someone will be little more difficult than selecting Mail from the File menu instead of Print, or dropping the document on an icon representing that user. It will also support encryption mechanisms for security authentication (so that you can make sure a message is coming from the person it says it is coming from). AOCE is slated for release late in 1993, and no pricing or distribution information was available at press time.

What Will QuickDraw GX Mean to You?

QuickDraw is the toolbox, or set of programming routines, in the Mac operating system that is responsible for displaying everything that you see on the screen and much of what gets printed on non-PostScript printers. The QuickDraw built in to every Mac has changed very little since the original Mac was released in 1984; the major change has been the addition of color to QuickDraw in 1988, and Color QuickDraw is built into every Mac that can support color monitors.

QuickDraw GX will be an important major upgrade to QuickDraw. Here's some of what it will give you:

Integrated Support for Type 1 PostScript Fonts

This means that Type 1 fonts will display on screen smoothly at all sizes without the use of Adobe Type Manager. Additionally, QuickDraw GX will support new capabilities in fonts, allowing developers to add features to their programs that will permit you to resize, rotate and slant type by dragging handles on its edges.

Consistent Color Management

Color has long been a problem for those who need to print it, as well as display it on screen, because there are several methods of specifying colors. There are also differences in how a color appears on screen and on a printer. QuickDraw GX is designed to provide a consistent color model for all devices connected to the Macintosh.

Enhanced Printer Capabilities

Beyond the addition of color matching, QuickDraw GX also will make it easier for printer manufacturers to write Mac software that supports those printers. For users, that means it will be easier to connect unusual printers. You will also be able to print in different ways, for example by dropping the icon of a document on to an icon of a printer (this last feature, by the way, was promised for the original release of System 7, but didn't make it). You will be able to stop print jobs in progress, and start them again from any page (or simply from where they left off) and preview them after they have been spooled to the printer.

New Graphics Power

Though applications will have to be rewritten to take advantage of them (developers are already working on it), QuickDraw GX adds more than 500 new system routines for displaying graphics. These routines will make Mac graphics programs more powerful and flexible.

QuickDraw GX will also let you create portable digital documents (PDDs)that can be viewed and printed by other Mac users, even if they don't have the software that created them.

QuickDraw GX is due to be released before the end of 1993. Apple has not announced *how* it will distribute the software, just that it will eventually be included as part of general System software releases.

PART
3

Printing and Fonts

The tips in this chapter are about printing and the ins and outs of selecting, installing, and using fonts.

The Ins and Outs of Installing the Print Driver

A *print driver* is software that tells the Mac how to communicate with a printer. Print drivers are stored in the Extensions folder and are called Chooser Extensions. The icon for the printer file usually looks something like the printer. This is, after all, the Mac.

When you buy a printer designed to be used with the Mac, it includes a disk containing the print driver. This disk should contain an Installer. If not, you can install the driver manually either by dragging it into the Extensions folder or dropping it onto the icon of the closed System Folder.

When you perform an Easy Install of System 7.1 with the Apple System Software disks, drivers for *all* Apple printers are placed in your Extensions folder. Likewise, preconfigured systems from Apple (specifically the Performas and the PowerBook 145B) come with all printer drivers installed. In most cases, you'll probably only have one or two of these printers, so you can safely trash the drivers for printers you do not have. To trash these files, drag them from the Extensions folder to the Trash icon.

How to Turn on Background Printing

Background printing is the feature that lets you continue to use the Mac while it is printing. Without background printing, the Mac is tied up from the time you ask it to print until the last page is printed.

Turn on background printing with the Chooser. If the printer you select supports background printing, the radio buttons that allow you to specify background printing are enabled, as shown here:

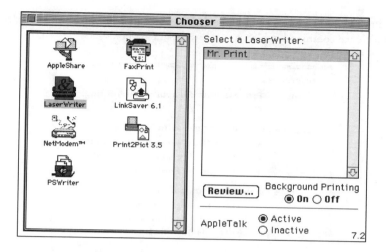

If the Background Printing radio buttons are *not* enabled for the printer you choose, chances are the driver for that printer does not support background printing. The manual that came with your printer should answer this question definitively.

How Background Printing Works

TIP 143

When background printing is turned on, the application does not send its printing instructions directly to the printer. Instead, the printer driver captures the output from the application and saves it as an intermediate file stored in the System Folder's PrintMonitor Documents folder. The Finder monitors the contents of this folder and when it sees that the application has closed the file (that is, when it has stopped printing to the intermediate file), it launches the PrintMonitor application. (The Installer places the PrintMonitor file in the Extensions folder in the System Folder.) When PrintMonitor starts, it immediately prints any documents inside that folder, in the order in which they were created.

How to Configure PrintMonitor

TIP 144

When something goes wrong with the printing process, PrintMonitor alerts you. The kinds of things that can go wrong include the printer running out of paper, a paper jam, and the printer not being available (for example, when it's turned off). You can configure PrintMonitor to alert you in one of three ways, as shown in the PrintMonitor Preferences dialog box.

To configure PrintMonitor, start it by double-clicking its icon in the Extensions folder. Choose the File menu's Preference command, which summons this dialog box:

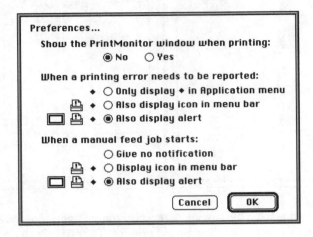

If you think you're going to be changing the PrintMonitor settings a lot, put an alias of it in the Apple Menu Items folder or some other easily accessible location.

How to Delay or Postpone Printing Using PrintMonitor

Sometime you may want to postpone a print job that you've already started. For example, you may have a very long document to print, but you don't want to tie up the office's shared printer with it during the business day when your coworkers may also have important documents to print. Print-Monitor lets you specify an exact time for a print job to start printing. Here's how:

1. Make sure Background printing is turned on, using the Chooser.

2. Print the document using the application's Print command.

3. Wait a moment until the PrintMonitor application starts (this usually takes five to ten seconds; check the Applications menu until its name appears) and then choose it from the Applications menu, as shown here:

If the print job is in progress—that is, if its name is listed in the top pane of the window—click the Set Print Time button to summon the Set Print Time dialog box, shown here. If the print job is listed only in the bottom pane, click the name to select it.

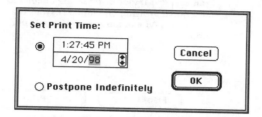

The Set Print Time dialog box lets you specify when a print job is to start. To set a specific time, click on any of the fields for time or date, which causes arrows to appear to the right of the time and date. Click the arrows up or down to set a new time or date; you can also type the new numbers directly. (The Postpone Indefinitely option lets you defer printing for an unlimited time, that is, until you later set a print time with the dialog box.)

If your Mac isn't on when a document is scheduled to print, the document is printed the next time you start it up; there is no alert.

If the printer is not turned on when the appointed time for a print job occurs, you are notified that the printer is not available, as shown here:

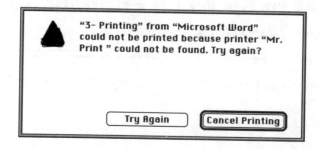

Shutting Down or Restarting with a Print Job in Process

If you shut down or restart your Mac while a print job is in progress, the Finder forces PrintMonitor to quit (you can't do this manually, as PrintMonitor doesn't have a Quit command). When this happens, PrintMonitor displays the following dialog box:

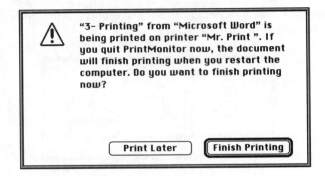

If you click the Finish Printing button, PrintMonitor continues to print, and the Mac does *not* restart or shut down when the print job is completed.

If you click the Print Later button, PrintMonitor quits, and the Mac restarts or shuts down; printing begins again when the Mac restarts. Note that even if the job has been partially printed, printing resumes from the *beginning* of the document when the Mac restarts, not from where it has left off when interrupted.

What to Do When PrintMonitor Needs More Memory

PrintMonitor works with as little as 80K of free memory although its default memory partition is 110K, as shown here:

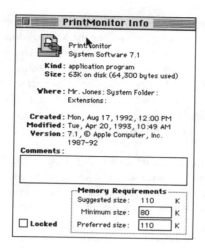

Sometime when it's printing a complicated document, PrintMonitor needs to use more memory than the default 110K of RAM. In this situation, PrintMonitor alerts you (the style of the alert depends on how you have told it to display alerts) that it needs more memory and asks if it should resize itself. If you acquiesce, it quits, adjusts the memory size it needs, and starts up again.

If you find this happening to you on a regular basis, you can use the Get Info window for PrintMonitor to adjust its preferred size permanently. If you do this, the Finder reserves this amount of memory for PrintMonitor if it is available; it reverts to a smaller amount of RAM if the specified amount is not available.

What Are the Different Kinds of Printers?

There are two basic kinds of printers: those that have the built-in PostScript page description language and those that do not. Those with PostScript are called, logically enough, PostScript printers. Those that don't include PostScript are called QuickDraw printers. Calling these printers QuickDraw is downright misleading because it's the Mac itself that provides the QuickDraw, not the printer.

We call them QuickDraw printers because they contain no internal page description language of their own. When the Mac prints to such a printer, it "merely" instructs the printer as to where on the page it should print every dot.

When you purchase a QuickDraw printer (that is, any printer without PostScript) make sure that it comes with the necessary cables and software to allow the Mac to speak to it; some discount stores sell inexpensive laser printers designed to be used with DOS systems, and generally do not come with Mac cables and software. If you're one of those hardy, adventurous souls who decides that an inexpensive non-Mac-specific laser printer is just the ticket, GDT of Vancouver, B.C., makes cables and software that allow the Mac to be connected to a wide variety of printers. Since you are by definition either extremely cost conscious, extremely poor, or both, take into account the cost of the hardware and software you'll need when you're evaluating such a printer.

PostScript printers, on the other hand, contain their own page description language, which the printer uses rather than the Mac's internal QuickDraw to create the page image. Basically, when printing, the Mac only needs to tell the printer to put, say, an A at a specific spot on the page, and what size to make the A. Instead of the Mac having to specify every dot that makes up the A, it just tells it to print an A.

Most PostScript printers include LocalTalk connectors for connecting the printer to the Mac. Furthermore, most PostScript printers work with Apple's LaserWriter driver, so it's not so necessary that you find special software (though many such printers do come with that software to take advantage of special features).

Why Leaving the Chooser Open Isn't Such a Good Idea

TIP 149

Don't leave the Chooser open with an icon such as a printer driver or AppleShare selected. In this condition, the Chooser constantly queries the network as to which resources are available, which adds unnecessary network traffic, which in turn can lead to poor network response. If you find it convenient to leave the Chooser open when you switch to other tasks, make sure none of the Chooser resource icons are selected when you switch.

System 6, 7, 7.1, and 8.0 Printer Drivers Can Coexist

TIP 150

Prior to System 7, it was necessary that all Macs on the same network use the same version of the System. The printer drivers that come with System 7, though, can work with System 6.0.7 and 6.0.8.

For these System 6 Macs, use the System 7.1 Installer to do a customized install that installs only the printer driver(s).

The Latest and Greatest: LaserPrinter Driver 8.0

In April 1993, Apple and Adobe jointly announced a new driver for PostScript printers. This driver, named PSPrinter 8.0, has several benefits, including:

❑ *Faster printing* Programs that do not generate their own PostScript code will print much faster, as the portion of the driver that translates Macintosh QuickDraw to PostScript operates much more quickly. However, many desktop publishing programs (such as QuarkXPress and versions of Aldus PageMaker prior to 5.0) *do* generate their own PostScript and thus do not benefit from this speed up. Both spooling to disk and printing from PrintMonitor are quicker.

❑ *More customizeability* The new printer driver uses separate PPD (PostScript Printer Description) files for different printers. This makes it easier to add new features, without necessitating the writing of an entire new driver.

❑ *Support for the enhanced capabilities of PostScript Level 2* If you have a printer with PostScript Level 2 built into it, you should upgrade.

❑ *More options when you save PostScript files on disk* These include options for specifying Encapsulated PostScript Files (EPS or EPSF) and limiting which fonts are stored in the PostScript file.

There are several ways to acquire the new driver. Adobe is selling it, along with PPD files for most PostScript printers, for $24.95. Call 1-800-83-FONTS (or, more precisely, 1-800-833-6687) for information or to order. If you have an Apple printer, you can also get the driver from your dealer or download it from online services. The manufacturer of your printer may also be able to provide it. In the future, new PostScript printers will have this driver included.

Quick Paper Size and Margin Reference in LaserWriter Driver 8.0

The new Version 8 printer driver has a handy way to see the selected paper size and margins. In the left portion of the Page Setup dialog box is a shaded area displaying the lower case letter a that Adobe uses as part of its logo. In the Apple version of the driver, the familiar dogcow is shown.

Click anywhere in this shaded area to change this display to the width and height of the paper and the four margins, as shown here:

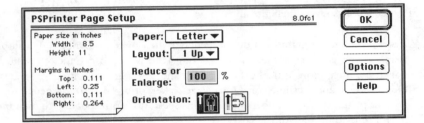

These measurements change to reflect your selections of paper size, layout, and orientation. Note that the measurements are in inches only, even if you use centimeters, picas, or another measurement scale in the application. Perhaps this oversight will be remedied in a later release of the driver—perhaps not.

Note that the four margins are *not* the margins specified in the software you are using; they represent the maximum area of the page on which the application can print. These settings vary from printer to printer. You can increase them by checking the Larger Print Area box in the Options dialog box.

Printing to a PostScript File with the Version 7 Printer Driver

Both the Version 7 and Version 8 PostScript printer drivers allow you to "print" directly to a PostScript disk file rather than to a printer. The Version 8 printer driver has some capabilities not available in Version 7; these are discussed separately.

Printing to a PostScript file is a good technique when you need to print a document on a different PostScript printer at a different site. An example of this is when you have created and proofed a document on your own printer, but plan to print it on a higher-resolution printer at a service bureau. If you take the original document file, you also need to ensure that the Macs at that location have the same fonts installed as your own Mac. Since a PostScript file contains within it the actual PostScript definitions of the fonts you are using, you can forget about these font-compatibility issues by printing to a PostScript file. Saving a PostScript file also makes it easier to deliver formatted documents to others (even on other types of computers) for printing.

PostScript files can be quite large, especially if they contain graphics or more than a few downloaded fonts. Using TrueType fonts also results in larger PostScript files. In addition to the description of the TrueType font itself, the PostScript file contains the "TrueType rasterizer," the PostScript instructions that tell a printer how to print those fonts.

To print to a PostScript file using the Version 7.*x* printer driver, click the PostScript file radio button in the Print dialog box, as shown here:

```
LaserWriter  "Mr. Print "                    7.2     [ Save ]
Copies: [1]        Pages: ● All  ○ From: [    ] To: [    ]   [ Cancel ]
 Paper Source
 ● All   ○ First  From: [ Cassette        ▼ ]    [ Options ]
          Remaining From: [ Cassette      ▼ ]

Destination:  ○ Printer        ● PostScript® File
Print Pages:  ● All  ○ Odd Pages Only   ○ Even Pages Only
Section Range: From: 1     To: 1        □ Print Selection Only
□ Print Hidden Text   □ Print Next File   □ Print Back To Front
```

The name of the Print button automatically changes to Save. This summons a standard Save file dialog box, asking you where to save the file and what to name it; the default name is PostScript.

Printing to a PostScript File with the Version 8 Printer Driver

The Version 8 printer driver gives you some additional capabilities, as mentioned earlier. The radio buttons for switching between printing to the printer and printing to a file are slightly different, as shown here:

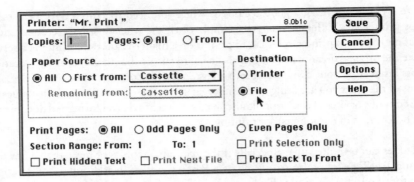

The Save button summons the Save dialog box, which contains some additional options, as shown here:

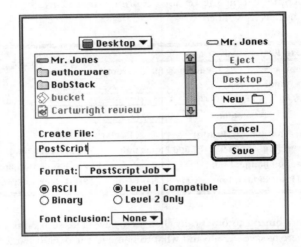

Typically you will choose the PostScript Job format, but you can also choose among several flavors of EPS (Encapsulated PostScript) formats. These formats all format the PostScript file to be saved in such a manner that other programs can work with it. For example, Adobe Illustrator and Aldus Freehand can edit EPS files, allowing you to import data into them that you might not otherwise be able to do.

The EPS Mac Standard Preview format includes a 72 dot-per-inch preview image of the file for displaying it on a Macintosh screen. Since this image cannot be edited when you place the EPS file into some other applications, it may become distorted when you attempt to resize it.

The EPS Mac Enhanced Preview format includes a PICT format as a preview for displaying the file. This version will provide a better preview of the file when edited in another application, but will also produce larger files.

EPS No Preview includes no preview image.

Note that EPS files are limited to *one page* in length. It is up to you—and the application you are using—to make sure the EPS file you create is no longer than a page. Use the Print Range radio buttons in the Print dialog to specify which page of a document you want to print. Also note, that many applications, especially those that work with graphics, include their own ways of saving EPS files; if that's the case, use the application's own facilities instead of printing to an EPS file.

Binary formatting results in smaller files, compared to ASCII formatting. If the final destination of a print job is a printer that includes Level 2 PostScript, you can choose to have those instructions embedded in the file.

Finally, the Save dialog box allows you to specify which fonts are included in the PostScript file. If you will always be using the PostScript file on the same Mac, you don't need to include fonts in the PostScript file. A good compromise, though, is to include all but the 13 fonts that are a standard feature of almost every PostScript printer.

For the record, note that Adobe's use of the word "fonts" is slightly at variance with standard Mac usage: a font means a particular style of a font, in addition to its "plain" style. Thus, the 13 fonts are Courier, Courier Bold, Courier Oblique, Courier Bold Oblique, Symbol, Helvetica, Helvetica Bold, Helvetica Oblique, Helvetica Bold Oblique, Times Roman, Times Bold, Times Italic, and Times Bold Italic.

Downloading Fonts to a Laser Printer

TIP 155

When you print a document that uses fonts that are not built into the printer, those fonts need to be downloaded to the printer each time the document is printed. Documents that contain fonts that must be downloaded take longer to print than those that contain only built-in printer fonts. In addition, downloading fonts to the printer increases the traffic on the network and therefore slows it down.

After a document with a downloaded font or fonts is printed, the downloaded fonts are purged from the printer's memory. This keeps the printer memory from filling up with fonts that it no longer needs. This is the up side of the downloadable fonts scheme. The down side is that the downloaded fonts are purged when the next document is printed, even if it contains the very fonts currently in memory. This inefficiency can be maddening if you experience it on a regular basis.

You can avoid this document-by-document downloadable font purging dilemma to some degree. Use Apple's LaserWriter Utility, which is supplied with each PostScript laser printer, to download Type 1 fonts to the printer so that they remain in the printer's memory until the printer is reset, turned off, or until the printer needs the memory used by these fonts for some other task, such as page imaging. You can also use a variety of third-party utilities. Our favorite is the LaserStatus desk accessory, which is part of CE Software's Widgets package.

If you don't know which built-in fonts your printer provides, you can find out by looking in the documentation that came with the printer (you probably keep the documentation readily accessible, just like we do).

Some Apple printers allow you to download TrueType fonts as well. Check your printer documentation to see if this is the case; if so, then the Apple LaserWriter Utility is the only program we know of that provides this function.

Which Fonts Print Faster?

If you're interested in the fastest printing possible, the guidelines are fairly simple. First, use only your printer's built-in fonts. Of these, the monospaced fonts (Courier, for example) print faster than proportionally spaced fonts.

If the printer is a PostScript printer, then Type 1 fonts will print faster than TrueType fonts; when you print a document containing a TrueType font, the PostScript software that allows it to print a TrueType font must be downloaded to the printer along with the document itself, and this adds to the time a print job takes to begin.

If your printer does not support PostScript, then all fonts print at the same speed.

Identifying Built-in Fonts in Your Laser Printer

The names of the fonts that are built into a PostScript printer aren't a big secret. The list is almost always found in the printer manual. The startup page often contains a list of the built-in fonts, in addition to such other scintillating information as the size of the RAM and the number of pages printed since birth (the printer's birth, not yours). Both Apple's LaserWriter Utility and CE Software's LaserStatus desk accessory will check any PostScript printer and give you a list of built-in fonts.

How to Deal with Corrupted Fonts

TIP 158

If the Mac is displaying garbage on the screen or if it's crashing during observable font-related activities, you may be experiencing the dreaded corrupted fonts syndrome. If you suspect that a font file has become corrupted, open it by double-clicking on the font's icon. (The font file icon is found in a suitcase file which is found in the System Folder's Fonts folder.) A corrupted font file will not open properly when you double-click it.

If you find that a font file is corrupted, reinstall it from a backup disk. The easiest way is to drop the replacement file icon onto the closed System Folder. System 7.1 will automatically place it in the System Folder's Fonts folder.

Aliases Don't Work in the Fonts Folder

TIP 159

Don't put aliases of font files in the Fonts folder. While logic implies that the alias should work, it doesn't. In System 7.1, font files must be in the Fonts folder for the system to make use of them (unless you are using a utility such as Suitcase or MasterJuggler to manage fonts).

Installing Fonts

TIP 160

You can install fonts by dropping their icons onto the icon of the closed System folder. If an application is open when you install fonts, it won't know about the new fonts until you restart it. That's because applications check for available fonts only when you launch them.

TIP 161

Removing Fonts from Your System

You can remove fonts from the system only when the sole open application is the Finder. Should you attempt to remove fonts from the Fonts folder (System 7.1) or the System file (System 7.0) while another application is running, the Finder alerts you to the fact that this is not allowed. As mentioned in the previous tip, applications only check for available fonts when they are first launched. Since the result of removing a font that an application thinks is available would probably be catastrophic, think of this bit of Finder-enforced discipline as a safety feature not unlike motorized seat belts—annoying but quite functional.

If disk space is at a premium, you can remove *all* fonts from the Fonts folder. Indeed, you can remove the Fonts folder itself. When the system restarts, a new, empty Fonts folder will be created automatically if it is not present.

The System file contains built-in bitmaps for 9- and 12-point Geneva, as well as 9-point Monaco. The ROMs in Macs newer than the Mac II also contain bitmaps for the 12-point Chicago font. Since the System can work with just these fonts, if disk space is at a premium, you can get rid of all the fonts. (When using System 7.0 and 7.1, even when you remove the icons for Geneva, Monaco, and Chicago from the System file, the sizes listed above actually remain in the system; they are hidden.)

With System 7.0, removing these fonts results in a smaller system file, thus freeing up more than 100K or so of RAM. You don't get this benefit with System 7.1.

TIP 162

TrueType and Small Bold

TrueType fonts generally do not display bold on the screen in sizes of 10 points or less. This can make determining formatting a bit cumbersome. To check whether or not small size TrueType text is bold, select it and check the application's text command menu (usually Style or Format).

Avoid Mixing Font Technologies

TIP 163

Even though System 7.0 and 7.1 both automatically install TrueType versions of Times, Helvetica, Symbol, and Courier fonts, it's prudent to remove them from the System file, leaving only the bitmap versions. This is especially true if you are using Adobe Type Manager. The system uses the TrueType version of the font for display, but the PostScript version for printing. In most cases, the differences between the two kinds of fonts are minor, but if you are doing exacting work, it is possible that line breaks will be different between the screen display and the printed document.

Since Courier is not a proportional font, the differences between the two versions are minor, so you can safely leave the TrueType version of Courier installed. This saves a little disk space since TrueType fonts do not require separate printer files. On the other hand, if you are creating documents destined for a high-end imagesetter, stick with the PostScript version.

Techniques for Making Font Suitcases

TIP 164

If you need to create a new suitcase, keep the following in mind.

First, some font management utilities—such as Suitcase II and MasterJuggler—include commands for creating a new empty suitcase. You can also create an empty suitcase by duplicating an existing one and removing its contents.

The Finder gives you two related techniques to make a copy of an existing folder; these two techniques are the same techniques available for making a copy of a file.

The first technique is to open the Fonts folder in the System Folder, select a font suitcase, and choose the File menu's Duplicate command. This results in a new suitcase with the same name as the original in the root directory of the System Folder.

The second technique is to OPTION-drag the icon of a font suitcase from the Fonts folder to another location, such as the desktop. With this command the Finder makes a copy of the original file with the same name.

Now that you've created a copy of a suitcase, you can rename it and then change it's contents. You can make it an empty suitcase by opening it and dragging its contents to the Trash.

How to Access the Symbol for the Command (⌘) Key

The Command key symbol (⌘) is available in the Chicago font. Should you need it in a document, set the font to Chicago and type CTRL-Q. In most other fonts, CTRL-Q is a nonprinting character.

Since the version of Chicago that's installed with System 7.1 is a TrueType font, you can type and print this character in any point size.

Getting Close to Ligatures

A *ligature* is a special single character that combines two characters. The Mac supports two ligatures, fi and fl, as shown here:

Ligature	Replaces	How to Type
fi	f i	SHIFT-OPTION-5
fl	f l	SHIFT-OPTION-6

Prudent use of ligatures can give some documents a more polished appearance than they would otherwise have.

How to Acquire Adobe Screen Fonts

Adobe makes bitmap versions of its entire font library available online free for the downloading. They can be found on CompuServe, in Library 10 of the Adobe Forum (GO: ADOBE). The fonts are oddly packaged (filenames are numbered, and don't relate to the names of the fonts they contain), so use CompuServe's searching software to locate the font you want.

Since Adobe is in business to sell products rather than give them away, these files do *not* contain the PostScript fonts necessary for printing on PostScript laser printers. But these screen fonts are very handy if you occasionally need to read documents that contain fonts that you don't own. However, fonts won't scale smoothly onscreen or when printed.

How to Circumvent the 128-Suitcase Limit in 7.1

System 7.1 permits a maximum of 128 font suitcases to be in the Fonts folder. This is half the maximum number of files that can be opened at a time on the Macintosh (256). This does *not* mean there is a limit of 128 fonts, however, as you can combine several fonts into a single suitcase.

The limit also does not mean that there can be only 128 items in the Fonts folder; PostScript printer font files do not count, as those files are only used when the font needs to be downloaded to the printer.

When organizing fonts into suitcases, consider combining them in logical groups. For example, all fonts built into the printer might be kept in one or two suitcases, and other suitcases may contain such things as display fonts, fonts related to a special project, or seldom-used fonts.

It's easier to manage groups of fonts if you keep all versions of the same font together in a suitcase. For example, keep the TrueType and bitmap versions of Bookman together in the same suitcase instead of breaking them apart.

The Correct Version of ATM to Use with System 7.1

Versions of Adobe Type Manager earlier than 3.0 are incompatible with System 7.1. They cannot find the PostScript versions of fonts (which are required for use with this program) if they are located in the Fonts folder. Instead, they search the Extensions folder for them. You can upgrade to version 3.0 of ATM by calling 1-800-521-1976, extension 440. The price for the 3.0 version is $7.50.

This offer, announced in October, 1991, is to remain in effect until Apple delivers system software that offers the same functionality as ATM. This software, called QuickDraw GX, is due to ship in late 1993.

Avoid Having TrueType and Type 1 Versions of the Same Fonts

Don't mix Type 1 (PostScript) and TrueType versions of the same font. We've heard reports of some applications becoming confused when they encounter both versions of the same font.

PART 4

Networks and Communication

To Save Memory, and for Better Security, Don't Leave File Sharing Turned On at All Times

It's not a good idea to leave File Sharing turned on by default: it uses about 256K of RAM. On Macs with 8Mb or less of RAM this 256K can make the difference between being able to keep all of the applications and DAs you want active and not being able to. Leaving File Sharing turned off as the default also makes security much easier to handle. Unless you have folders on your disk that others rely on, turn File Sharing on only when it's needed.

What's Program Linking and Why You Should Leave It Turned Off

Program Linking, which can be enabled on the Sharing Setup control panel, allows programs on other machines, connected to yours on a network, to send instructions (in the form of Apple events) to programs running on your machine. This has the effect of giving users on other machines at least partial control over programs running on yours. While its use is limited for the time being, more and more programs are compatible with Apple events, meaning that more and more programs can react to events coming over the network.

To make sure that no one on the network can control your machine, simply make sure you do not start Program Linking. If you *do* have it running, make sure that you use the Users and Groups control panel to carefully limit the users to whom you grant this privilege.

Use an Alias to Make Turning File Sharing On and Off More Convenient

To make Sharing easier to turn off and on, place an alias of the Sharing Setup control panel in your Apple Menu Items folder or in your main aliases folder on the desktop. This lets you avoid the steps of opening the control panels folder and locating the control panel to turn it off and on.

Develop Guest Privileges Street Smarts

Anyone on the network can mount one of your shared volumes if you've allowed Guest Privileges. While guest access is handy, it does represent a possible security breach. It's not unlike leaving the door to your big-city apartment unlocked all the time—convenient but not too smart. By default, guest access is turned off when the System is installed. Don't turn it on without carefully evaluating how you'd feel about the information in your files becoming fodder for Oprah or Donahue.

Make Aliases of Frequently Used Network Volumes

Keep aliases of network volumes that you use often in a place where they are easy to get to, such as your Alias folder on the desktop, or your Apple Menu Items folder. With the alias, you can open the network volume directly, without having to wade through the Chooser.

See Tip 177 about zones and network volume aliases.

Copy Files to and Mount a Network Volume with One Click and Drag

If you have an alias of an unmounted network volume on your desktop, you can both copy files to the volume and mount the volume in one step. Drag the file or files to the network volume alias. The volume first mounts (you'll be asked for a password if one is required); then the copying will begin.

Network Zones and Volume Aliases

As handy as the trick of using an alias to mount a network volume is, it might not work if your network is divided into zones and you mount volumes from each zone. When you open the volume alias, it will mount automatically only if its zone is the zone you last accessed. If you last accessed another zone, the Finder displays an alert box proclaiming that the volume you've requested is not available. Life is hard when your cool new Mac trick doesn't work the way you expected.

Don't Launch Applications on a Network Volume

To keep network traffic to a minimum, don't launch applications that are on a network volume. Besides creating a lot of unnecessary traffic, it is an exercise in frustration because it takes a very long time for the application to load. You might be able to tolerate this situation if you only need to launch the application occasionally. If you need to launch the application more often, install it on your local hard disk. As an alternative, you might be able to open it with an application you do have installed on your local hard disk that can translate the file.

Remember, you must be licensed for each application you use. It's both a good idea and the law.

How to Select and Use Passwords Safely

Networks identify you both by the name under which you log in and the password you use. Most people probably know your name, but you should take steps to make your password harder to figure out, and then change it often. Here are some suggestions:

❑ Avoid using a password that can be figured out independently. Examples of this include your middle name, the names of your spouse or children, and your birth date. That old standby of banks—your mother's maiden name—is not a bad idea, especially if it is also accompanied by an additional character or two. The more characters in a password, the harder it is for others to guess. Mix punctuation in with letters (passwords are case sensitive).

❑ Avoid using the same password for all of your network connections and services (including online services).

❑ Don't write any of your passwords down and put them on post-it notes on your monitor!

❑ Finally, change your passwords often—say, every month or two.

Don't Share What You Don't Want Others to See

If there are folders on your hard disk that you absolutely do not want others to see, the best strategy is to make sure those folders are not shared (and that they are not contained by folders that are shared). This means you should not share your entire hard disk if there are folders on that hard disk you want hidden; instead share only those folders you really want others to see.

Put Away Network Volumes When Finished with Them

When you have finished with a network volume, unmount it by either using the Finder File menu Put Away or dragging it to the Trash.

By disconnecting from network volumes, you reduce the amount of traffic on the network, and thereby help to maintain its overall efficiency.

Why Ten Shared Folders Is Enough

System 7 File Sharing allows you to share up to ten separate folders at once. When you attempt to share more folders than this, the Finder warns you that you cannot share more folders.

This limit does not include folders within folders. When you share a folder, by default all the folders within that folder have the same set of access privileges as the parent folder. You, or anyone else who has access privileges that allow them, can change the privileges for individual folders separately.

Finding Out Which Folders Are Shared with the File Sharing Monitor

Use the File Sharing Monitor control panel to determine which folders are currently shared. There are no characteristics of a folder that you can search for using the Finder Find command.

When folders are shared, the File Sharing Monitor control panel displays a scrolling list of the folders being shared, as shown here:

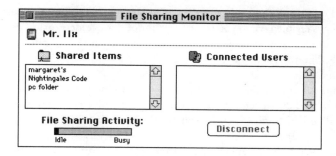

If you regularly need to verify which folders are being shared, position this control panel so it is at the bottom part of the screen. This technique can also help you navigate quickly to a deeply nested shared folder. After you've determined the name of the shared file from the File Sharing Monitor list, use its name in the Name field of the Finder's Find dialog box.

You can also assign a specific label to folders you are sharing. Use the Labels control panel to name one of the labels Shared, and when you share a folder, use the Label menu to attach that label to a shared folder. You can use the expanded More Choices version of the Finder's Find dialog box to search for folders with specific labels.

Turn Off File Sharing to Rename a Volume

A volume that is shared or contains folders that are shared cannot be renamed while File Sharing is turned on. Turn File Sharing off with the Sharing Setup control panel first. The exception to this rule is floppy disks. Since they cannot participate in the file sharing game, floppy disks can be renamed whenever you like, regardless of the status of File Sharing.

File Sharing and Removable Disks

Using File Sharing with removable disks (such as Syquest, Bernoulli, and magneto-optical) requires special considerations.

First, you cannot share any removable volume you mount after File Sharing is turned on. That means that if File Sharing is enabled when you boot, you cannot share folders on any removable volume that you insert later. The somewhat cumbersome workaround is to turn File Sharing off, mount the volume, and then turn File Sharing back on.

Second, you cannot eject or unmount (Put Away) any removable volumes that were mounted when File Sharing was turned on—even if nothing on that volume is shared. For this problem Apple has a small program called UnMount It that is available through the usual online sources.

Both of these problems, however, *can* be solved with a separate utility called DriveShare from Casablanca Software.

None of the above, by the way, applies to floppy disks, since they can't be shared.

The Coolest and Most Underpublicized System Software Apple Sells Is AppleTalk Remote Access (ARA)

AppleTalk Remote Access (ARA) is a communications program from Apple that lets you connect via modem to any Mac or AppleTalk network. But that somewhat mundane description hides the magic of the product—magic that can free you to work at home, or, if you have a PowerBook, from wherever you can find a phone line. That's because when you connect with ARA you can do everything you can do when connected by LocalTalk or other network connections. This includes accessing network servers and other shared volumes, printing to network printers, and using electronic mail. Even if you have a single solitary Mac at the office, you can use ARA to dial in to access files anytime you want.

Quit AppleTalk Remote Access Once You Make Your Connection

AppleTalk Remote Access (ARA) has a recommended memory partition of 230K. After your connection is established, you can quit the application without affecting the connection. If memory is constrained on your Mac— for example, if you use one of the tens of thousands of 4Mb PowerBooks

Apple has sold—, those 240K of memory can make the difference between being able to run another application or not.

Let AppleTalk Remote Access Remind You of Its Connection Periodically

You can have ARA remind you of your connection as frequently as you like. Check the "Remind me of my connection" box in the main document window. You can specify in minutes how often you want to be reminded. The reminder is the dialog box shown below:

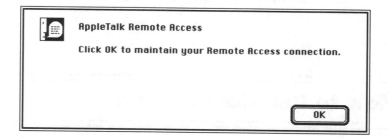

AppleTalk Remote Access

Click OK to maintain your Remote Access connection.

OK

ARA continues to notify you even if you quit ARA to free up memory (see Tip 187 about quitting ARA and keeping your connection). You will especially appreciate the reminder if you're incurring long-distance toll charges or if you're connected to a single-line system that others might also need to access remotely.

Now Is a Good Time to Get a Modem

If you don't have a modem, it's time to get one; prices for high-performance modems have never been lower, and the choice of online services has never been better. Besides several thriving, large, commercial services such as CompuServe, Prodigy, America Online, the Well, and AppleLink; special support systems such as the Berkeley Mac Users Group Planet BMUG system; and global networks such as the Internet, there are literally thousands of small Bulletin Board Systems (BBSs, for which no one has found a good plural). The range of information you can access on these systems and the number of people you can meet is nearly unlimited. These many online offerings form a critical part of the information age.

TIP 190 — Choosing a Commercial Online Service

As to which commercial service to use, we haven't had experience with all of them. CompuServe Information (CIS), with which we are most familiar, is the largest of the systems, but America Online seems to be growing quickly. Prodigy, whose software is still primitive and slow by Mac standards, also has its adherents. We use CompuServe because, for us, that's where the action is.

TIP 191 — How to Use CompuServe

We'd be remiss if we didn't point out that the CompuServe user interface is a menu-driven nightmare. Fortunately, there are two front-end applications that can shield you from most of the CIS ugliness: the CompuServe Navigator (from Michael C. O'Connor) and CompuServe Information Manager (from CompuServe Information Service).

These two products take different approaches to simplifying CompuServe. Navigator lets you choose the locations within CompuServe you wish to browse and the message areas and file libraries you wish to browse. When you have made your choices, you tell Navigator to run the session, and it dials CompuServe and performs all the tasks you specified, without your intervention. You can then review the "session file" and respond to messages, instruct the program to download files, and do other tasks; and the next time you run the session, Navigator will again perform the tasks you requested. We like Navigator because it doesn't require baby-sitting. CompuServe Information Manager, on the other hand, provides a more Mac-like environment, in which CompuServe services are presented to you using icons for different locations. This makes it much easier to wend your way through the CompuServe maze, but at the expense of requiring your attention.

What to Look for in a Modem

Modem prices have dropped dramatically recently. If you have been waiting, now is the time to take the leap. If you have an older 2400 bps modem, now is a good time to upgrade.

Mail-order and street prices of modems that operate at 14.4K bps, offer FAX, and include software and cables are less than $400.

When shopping for a modem, consider the usual facts about the vendor (type of support, warranty, and so on). Here are some other things you should look at as well:

Speed

Look for a modem that offers *at least* 14.4K bps (bits per second) operation. Modems of this type carry the designation v.32bis and will communicate well with modems that are also designed to that specification. Modems of this type also work at 2400 and 9600 bps. Not all online services and BBSs work at speeds greater than 9600 bps, but more and more do.

Fax Capabilities

You may already have a fax machine, but using a modem with built-in fax capabilities (almost all modems sold now include fax) offers several advantages. Most fax software allows you to fax a document directly from within any application from which you can print. This saves you the steps of printing and then feeding the printed document into a traditional fax machine—and with a fax modem, the faxes that you send and receive can be stored on disk for tidy storage and rapid retrieval.

Bundled Software

If the modem includes bundled software, check with knowledgeable users to ensure that it has some value before you factor it into your purchase decision. Many fax modems include the FAXstf fax software from stf Technologies, and all Global Village fax modems include GlobalFax software. We use both and they are very good.

Cables

High-speed modems usually require more sophisticated cables than slower 2400 bps modems. If the modem you are considering requires a special cable, verify that the correct cable is included with the modem.

Software Requirements

If you are using software that requires a special file to work properly with each brand of modem (for example, AppleTalk Remote Access needs specific files), contact the vendor to make sure it can supply you with the proper file for the modem you're considering.

Choose a Winner

Sometimes it's better to go with a proven performer than risk the unknown just to save a few dollars. We know of one international company that spent weeks in a failed attempt to get Macs on either side of the Atlantic to communicate reliably. When it replaced the modems on each end with a known performer in its class, the communications problems were solved almost immediately—the company was able to resume the business of earning a profit.

The Basics of File Compression

Many, if not most, of the files available on online services are compressed. Compression is a technique by which all the information in a file is reduced as much as possible. This makes the file smaller so it is faster to transfer over the modem line. There are several packages available for compressing files, most notably the StuffIt family of products. Before uploading files to an online service, make yourself familiar with the standards of that service regarding compression; some prefer that you create self-extracting archives (see Tip 194), while others prefer that you use another format such as the standard StuffIt format. AppleLink, for example, has its own compression standard, and it's good manners to use that format when uploading files to AppleLink.

Common Filename Extensions and What They Mean to You

Other computers, including PCs, usually use filename extensions as part of their filenames to let you (and programs) know what kind of file it is. Filename extensions are usually three characters long and appear at the end of a filename, after a period.

Filename extensions and the System 7 Extensions are totally unrelated subjects.

While Mac filenames sometimes have extensions, they are more common on DOS and UNIX systems. Here are some common extensions you're likely to see when visiting the online world.

.sit

This extension is produced by the StuffIt family of products, denoting compressed files. You can decompress these files using the free program StuffIt Expander. You can create them with the full StuffIt Deluxe 3.0 package or with the shareware StuffIt Lite software.

There have been several upgrades to the StuffIt line; if you have an older copy of the software (dated before 1991), it will not be able to extract files from the newer archives. StuffIt Expander and StuffIt Lite can be found in most of the usual online and shareware sources.

.sea

This extension stands for *self-extracting archive.* This means that the file is an application program containing a compressed file. You can double-click the files icon to open it, and usually a dialog box lets you choose where to save the file.

Both StuffIt and Compactor Pro can create .sea files.

.cpt

Files bearing this extension are produced by Bill Goodman's CompactPro program. StuffIt Expander, in addition to CompactPro, can read these files.

.dd

Files with this extension are fairly rare, and are produced by the DiskDoubler compression application. A public domain decompressor for these files, called DD Expand, is available.

.pit

This is an old standard, not likely to be seen much anymore. Files with the .pit extension were created by PackIt, the first popular Mac file compressor. StuffIt Deluxe can read these files.

.pkg

Files with this extension are created by AppleLink and its built-in package compression. In addition to AppleLink, StuffIt Deluxe and StuffIt Extractor can decompress these files.

.zip

The .zip files are created on MS-DOS systems by PKZIP. StuffIt Deluxe can translate and decompress these files. There are also some public domain and shareware utilities that can unzip these files.

.exe

The .exe files are DOS program files, and cannot be run on the Macintosh. Files with this extension are rarely found on online services, but they do occur. For the Mac user, they are mostly interesting when the uploader of the file has created a self-extracting package. If you find a self-extracting file with the .exe extension, you'll have to transfer it to a DOS machine for decompression.

.com

The .com files are smaller executable DOS files that generally contain commands. Handle these files as you would .exe files.

.z

This extension denotes a UNIX compressed file. StuffIt Deluxe 3.0 can read these files. This is useful if you are getting files from a UNIX-using colleague.

.hqx

Files with this extension have been through the BinHex process. Many other computers cannot deal with the binary data that the Mac typically uses. Generally, such things as sounds, pictures, programs, compressed files, and so on are binary files. Therefore, a routine called BINHEX (binary to hexadecimal) is used to translate the binary file to a text file. The reverse process is then used to change the text file into a binary file. For more details, see Tip 195.

StuffIt Deluxe, StuffIt Expander, and a variety of single-purpose utilities can read and translate to or from this format.

Note that .hqx files are typically much larger than their binary counterparts.

.gif

This file format was created by CompuServe to both compress files and facilitate use of graphics files by users with different kinds of computers.

Some Mac graphics applications can deal with .gif files. ClarisWorks can read .gif files, and Adobe PhotoShop can both read and write this format.

If you don't have PhotoShop and don't want to invest in it, a good choice is Kevin Mitchell's GifConverter. This Freeware program can read .gif files, and save them to the more standard (on the Mac) PICT format. GifConverter can also read PICT files and save them to the .gif format for uploading to various services. CompuServe Navigator can also open .gif files, but cannot save them in other formats.

The .gif format is not the format of choice for saving graphics files on the Mac for several reasons. It works with pictures stored only in 256 colors (8 bits per pixel). That's not that big a deal, but many Mac graphics have more colors. Files stored in the .gif format are much slower to open than other file formats with most Mac applications.

.jpg

Files with this extension are graphics files compressed using the standard JPEG conversion routines. See Part 2 for more details about JPEG files.

JPEGView, available on most online services, can read .jpg files, as can Adobe PhotoShop.

.txt

These files are usually text documents, with no formatting. All Mac word processors can read these files, as can TeachText and several other editors.

What Is the MacBinary Format and Why This Business About Two Forks in (Almost) EVERY File?

The MacBinary format is a solution to the Mac file fork problem. Most Macintosh files are composed of two portions called *forks:* the Resource fork and the Data fork. This dual nature of files is unique to the Macintosh, and if there were no way to combine them, other computer systems would mangle Mac files when they encountered them. MacBinary encases both forks, along with information about the file (date created, file type and creator, and so on) into a single file for use by other operating systems.

Almost all Mac communications programs support MacBinary. When you're transferring Mac files to another kind of computer, be sure to enable MacBinary (it is enabled by default in most programs). Other than that, the process is transparent: when a file is uploaded it is turned into a MacBinary file by the uploading application; when a MacBinary file is downloaded from another kind of computer, the communications software translates MacBinary, so the file appears with the correct icon, and both forks are joined together properly.

The only time you need to worry about MacBinary is when you download a Mac file to a PC. Since PC software doesn't know what to do with the MacBinary header information, the file stays together, and doesn't have the correct date and time of creation, file type or creator, and so on when it is copied to a Mac. For this situation there is a public domain program available called MacBinary (logically enough) that can decode the files. StuffIt Deluxe will do this for you also.

It's important to note that not all Mac files need to be encoded with MacBinary; if the file does not contain a resource fork (most data files do not contain a resource fork), then there's no reason for MacBinary. Fortunately, most telecommunications programs know about this and don't force a file without a resource fork to include one.

BinHex and Binary Files

Many communications services, such as Internet mail, do not permit binary files to be sent. (A binary file is one in which all 256 possible characters in an 8-bit byte are used.) Instead, they only permit 7-bits of a byte to be used. Since most Mac files are binary files and use all the data they can, this presents a problem.

The answer is BinHex—binary to Hexadecimal encoding (pronounced *bine-hex*). In this scheme, the data in a binary file is mapped to the equivalent data using 7-bit bytes. The file usually has the type of TEXT, and can be sent over virtually all online services. There are shareware and public domain encoders and decoders for the BinHex format, and the old standby StuffIt Deluxe (as well as Bill Goodman's Compact Pro) can both encode and decode BinHex files. The standard extension for a BinHex file is .hqx.

A BinHex file is usually much larger than the binary file, typically by about a third. Thus, a file that is 60K in binary form will balloon to about 80K in BinHex form. Before resorting to using BinHex, make sure the service you are using cannot accept regular binary files.

BinHex is kind of a superset of MacBinary, in that MacBinary information about file type and creator, as well as creation date and so on is included in the BinHex file.

Inside the Communications ToolBox

TIP 197

The Communications ToolBox is a set of tools residing in the System Folder. These tools, provided by Apple, allow programmers to use standard communications features, such as terminal emulation, downloading files, and the like without having to reinvent the wheel themselves. Additionally, developers can write new tools for use by the ToolBox, thus allowing all applications that support the ToolBox to use those tools. It also provides a standard user interface for those tasks.

The Communications ToolBox is included with those programs that require it. Apple sometimes makes updates to the ToolBox available, along with new tools, as they did with version 1.1 in January 1993. This version is available online.

If your system has the Communications ToolBox installed, you will see a file called CTB Resources in the top (root) level of the System Folder of your hard disk. Other resources used by the ToolBox are installed in the Extensions Folder. These files are called *communications extensions* and include files such as Apple Modem Tool (which includes instructions the ToolBox uses to communicate with various modems) and various tools for handling file transfer protocols (see Tip 198, next, about ZTerm). When you install the Communications ToolBox, several fonts used for terminal emulation are also installed in the Fonts folder.

ZTerm: It May Be the Perfect Basic Communications Program

If you don't have communications software, we recommend the $30 shareware package ZTerm. ZTerm, by David Alverson, is available from most user groups and online services. It's a nearly no-frills communications program that works well and swiftly and is easy to use.

Download Files to a Closed Folder to Save a Little Time and Money

Most communications programs allow you to specify the folder to which downloaded files are saved. Your downloads will be slightly more efficient (faster) if you keep this folder closed. It takes a few moments for the Finder to add the new file to the list of files in the window if the folder is open, and this can have an adverse (though admittedly small) effect on the downloading speed. If you pay a per-minute connection charge and often download many small files, you'll save entire cents over the course of a month.

Turn off Virtual Memory When Downloading Large Files or Downloading Frequently

Virtual memory, even when it isn't being used (that is, when the Mac isn't paging to disk), slows downloading. If you are going to be doing a lot of downloading, turn off Virtual Memory and restart your Mac. The improvement in download performance is substantial at 14.4K bps, but isn't as noticeable at 2400 bps.

Downloading in the Background Is Less Efficient

TIP 201

If your communications program is downloading a file in the background and you are simultaneously doing other work in a foreground application, then the speed at which it can download is reduced. This doesn't impact 2400 bps downloads as much as it does 9600 bps or 14.4K bps downloads. Some programs, too, affect the download speed more than others: calculation- or disk-intensive programs require more of the Mac's resources than a word processor spending most of its time waiting for you to type more characters. On the other hand, even word processors can slow a background file transfer while performing such tasks as spelling checks.

Reading PC Floppy Disks on the Mac

TIP 202

All Mac models introduced since late 1988 use the SuperDrive floppy disk drive, which can read PC disks. In addition to supporting both 800Kb and 1.44Mb Mac file formats, the SuperDrive, with the proper utility software, supports 3.5-inch DOS disks.

The System software installation kit includes an application called Apple File Exchange (AFE). AFE translates files from DOS to Mac formats as it copies them to your hard disk. However, AFE is not the most straightforward utility for this task.

There are three programs that allow the Mac to work more directly with DOS disks (that is, allow them to appear on the desktop). These are Apple's PC Exchange, Insignia Solutions' AccessPC, and Dayna's DOSMounter. They also let you format DOS disks in the SuperDrive and let you map DOS file extensions to Mac file types. All are reliable. Apple's PC Exchange is based on code provided by Insignia Solutions, and offers a subset of the AccessPC features.

AccessPC and DOSMounter have the added advantage of letting you read removable cartridges formatted on DOS systems. We've used all of these products for some time and we have no discernible preference among them.

Reading Mac Floppy Disks on the PC

203

With a shareware application called MacSee, PCs can read Macintosh 1.44Mb disks. MacSee is an interactive program, meaning that it does not mount Mac disks to the PC, so that you cannot address them from DOS as drive A: or B:; instead, it gives you a menu you can use to see the files on the Mac disk and copy them to your hard disk.

MacSee is a $35 shareware product from ReeveSoft of Clemson, South Carolina and is available from the usual sources.

The Rules for Naming DOS Files

204

Mac filenames can be up to 31 characters long, and can include any character except the colon. DOS systems have more stringent limitations: filenames can be composed of up to eight initial characters, followed by a period and an optional three-character extension, and there are enough forbidden characters to fill a good-sized table.

If you are sharing files with a DOS machine, be careful how you name your files. Name the file following DOS naming standards and conventions. See Tip 205, next, to learn the ins and outs of letting the Mac automatically assign DOS filenames to Mac files.

See a Preview of How DOS Users See Your Shared Mac Filenames

205

The Mac can translate Mac filenames to DOS for you automatically. With File Sharing turned on, you can see what the name of the file would be as seen by DOS users:

1. Make sure File Sharing is on.

2. Select the shared file in the Finder.

3. Press ⌘-I, or use the File Menu's Get Info command.

4. Click on the name of the file in the Get Info window. The name is now displayed as it will appear to DOS users, as shown here:

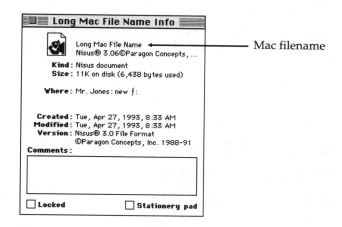

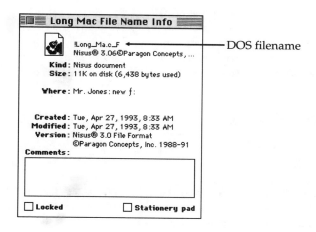

How the Mac Goes About Assigning DOS Names to Mac Files

When the Mac translates a long filename to a DOS-compatible filename, it places an exclamation point at the beginning of the filename. Next it replaces any spaces in the filename with underscores. It then uses the first seven characters of the Mac filename, including underlines and the exclamation point, to create the DOS filename. If the Mac filename already has a three-character extension, that is used. Otherwise, characters 8 through 10 of the Mac filename are used as the extension in the DOS filename.

Mac and Windows Have Different Character Sets

The Mac and Windows differ in how characters are encoded. Both systems use the same codes for the most common characters (those through ASCII values 128), but special characters—such as foreign characters with accent marks—are encoded differently. If you use translation software to move files between the two systems, the translation software takes care of remapping those different characters. If you move ASCII text files between the two machines without translation software, the characters are not translated, and any text in which you use foreign characters or many mathematical symbols are garbled.

Additionally, Windows does not support a few useful Mac characters. These characters are shown here:

$$\neq, \infty, \leq, \geq, \Sigma, \Pi, \pi, \Omega, \sqrt{}, \int, \approx, \Delta, \Diamond, \text{fi, fl}$$

Although these characters are defined in PostScript, Microsoft chose not to make them part of the standard Windows character set. Even a translation program can't help, so avoid using these characters in documents you intend to share with Windows users.

The standard character set used by DOS-based programs (that is, those that don't run in Windows) is even more limited. Due to its origins as a text-based environment, DOS uses many ASCII characters as "graphic" characters for line drawing. When you import documents containing these characters from DOS programs, the results are likely to be unpleasant.

Use the Mac and Windows Versions of the Same Application, If Possible, to Make Sharing Document Files as Simple as Possible

If you often trade files between the PC and the Mac, try, if possible, to standardize on the same programs on both machines. For example, for word processing there are sister versions of both Microsoft Word and WordPerfect on the Mac and the PC. Other mainstream programs that feature the same, or nearly the same functionality on both machines include Microsoft Excel, Claris FileMaker Pro and ClarisWorks, Lotus 1-2-3, Microsoft FoxBase, Aldus PageMaker, Aldus Persuasion, Microsoft PowerPoint, and MacroMedia's AuthorWare.

File Formats to Use When No Translators Are Available

More and more modern applications are equipped with the ability to read and write the most common file formats. But that doesn't mean you'll never be confronted with the need to export a Mac file to an application for which no translator is available. If you find yourself in this predicament, you can usually extricate yourself by using one of the lowest-common-denominator formats. (If you need an uncommon format more than occasionally, see Tip 210 for information about commercial translators.) Translating a file into one of these formats strips away everything but the text of your original file, but it's still much better than having to enter everything into the target application manually.

These formats are supported by almost every application that deals with text or tabular data.

Text

This format, also called ASCII, includes only the text you type into a program; no formatting (except for tabs and returns) is retained after a text translation.

Tab or Comma-delimited

Delimited files are used to transfer tabular data, the kind contained in spreadsheets and databases. In the Tab delimited format, each record in a database and each row in a spreadsheet, ends with a return, thus producing a single line for each record or row. Within that line, fields and columns are separated from one another by Tab characters. With the comma-delimited format, fields or columns are separated from one another by commas; since commas can be included *within* the data, quotation marks are placed around the fields (so a truer term for it would be quote-and-comma-delimited format).

This format does not retain the ancillary information that might be contained within a spreadsheet or a database. For example, it does not include the formula that might be part of a cell or field definition.

In addition to being a means of transferring tabular data between platforms, these formats are also used to move data between applications running on the same machine. For example, most word processors require text in one of these delimited formats for mail merging.

Other Table Formats

Some other formats for tabular data include the SYLK and DIF formats. These formats can be saved and read by many spreadsheets. However, they are quite old (dating to 1985) and don't include support for all the features of modern spreadsheets and databases.

Graphics Formats

While there are several common graphics formats, none really qualifies as a surefire format for use when transferring graphics between the Mac and the PC. For bitmap graphics, you can use CompuServe's GIF format (though it is limited to 256 colors), EPS, or TIFF. Check the software you are using to determine which formats are supported by both programs or use DeBabelizer, mentioned in Tip 210.

Recommended File-Translation Utilities

Although most modern programs can read and write the most common file formats, you might still need access to a file format that your application doesn't support directly. Here are some utilities that help you cover all the file-translation bases.

MacLinkPlus/PC

The DataViz MacLinkPlus/PC file translator package is probably the most popular product of its kind. MacLinkPlus/PC Version 7.1 includes Apple's Macintosh Easy Open utilities, discussed later. MacLink Plus/PC can translate between dozens of file formats on each machine. It can also serve as a communications link between the Mac and the PC (and includes a cable for connecting them). Many of its translators can also work directly with Microsoft Word 5.*x*, and it includes a bridge to the Claris XTND system (discussed in Tip 211). MasterSoft (The Software ToolWorks) also offers Word for Word Macintosh, a rich set of robust translators. If DataViz doesn't have the translator you need, or you find that the translator it offers doesn't translate specific features you need, Word for Word Macintosh is an excellent alternative.

DeBabelizer

This utility, from Equilibrium of Sausalito, California, is a must-have if you translate graphics between the Mac and the PC (or, as a matter of fact, between the Mac and virtually any other desktop personal computer, such as a Sun Workstation or Amiga). It can read and write the file formats of literally dozens of different programs. Best of all, it can alter the color lookup tables a picture uses (necessary for formats that do not support 24-bit true color) and dither files so they look good in those formats. Furthermore, it is scriptable, so you can tell it to apply the same set of transformations to all the files in a folder or to all the frames of a QuickTime movie.

Macintosh Easy Open

Macintosh Easy Open is an extension/control panel combination created by Apple. As noted earlier, it comes with the 7.1 version of MacLink Plus/PC, and will also come with other file-translation programs in the future. In short, Macintosh Easy Open provides an interface that lets files be translated without you opening a specific translation program. This software is discussed in more detail in Part 2.

Where to Get Additional XTND Translators

XTND is a file translation system developed by Claris and is used in almost all of the popular word processing products (except Microsoft Word and Microsoft Works). Products that use XTND include some filters for translating specific files. MacWrite Pro, for example, ships with over 50 translators. DataViz offers an even larger selection of file translation filters. If you require a translation filter for an obscure format, check with DataViz.

System Tips

Make Friends with Your System by Reading the Manual

Apple and the multitudes of enthusiastic Mac users would have you believe that setting up and using the Mac is as natural as falling out of bed, and not nearly as dangerous. While this is undoubtedly true, especially compared with other computers you might consider (or be forced into) using, if you don't know the basics, things can get a little complex. In fact, you might identify with those people you see in Mac ads struggling to configure Windows. If you're new to the Mac or to System 7.1, the best advice we can give is to read the manual. It's far from perfect and far from complete, but it's a good introduction, and it's free.

Choose System Version 7.1

There are too many versions of the system software. Some briefly served a purpose before becoming obsolete. Others arrived in the delicate condition sometimes referred to as "unstable" by polite society. In this context, unstable means it doesn't work. Fortunately for us all, there's a simple solution to this quandary, and it's called System 7.1. There are several reasons why we think version 7.1 is your best bet.

First, System 7.1 is the most stable version of Mac operating system to come out of Apple's software labs in some time. It's not rock solid, except when compared to previous versions.

System 7.1 is also a more *modular* version of the operating system than any of its predecessors. As mentioned later in the discussion of Enablers, System 7.1 can be tailored to new Macs with the simple addition of a small file in the System Folder. This alone makes system management much easier, particularly for those responsible for managing a mix of Mac models.

Beyond adding support for new machines, System 7.1 also makes it easier for Apple to add new capabilities, such as AppleScript and Apple Open Collaboration Environment (AOCE). System 7.1 is the backbone for Apple's strategy for upgrading the operating system until the next major revision of the operating system.

Acquiring System 7.1: Upgrades vs. Fresh Starts

System 7.1 is the first version of the operating system Apple has asked you to pay for. It is available in two flavors, an upgrade package, which is available directly from Apple, and the full package, which is available from any authorized Apple reseller, such as your local dealer. You can order the upgrade package directly from Apple by calling (800) 769-APPL (2775). When Apple initiated this upgrade procedure, it used to quiz you to make sure you were really already running some version of the Mac operating system. The questions were usually along the lines of "What colors are the stripes in the Apple in the menu bar?". The charge for this upgrade is $34.95 plus $3.00 for shipping. This package comes with very little documentation. If you want the complete System 7.1 documents, you'll have to buy the complete release at the higher price.

If you're already familiar with System 7.0, then the upgrade package (along with this book) will give you all the documentation you need. If you're upgrading from System 6 and have never used System 7, then you should buy the full package, with all the documents.

Updating from a Previous Version of the System

Installing a system on a disk for the first time is relatively simple: you insert the installation floppy disk, open the installer application, select the target disk, and click OK. (You only have to select the target disk if the Mac has more than one hard disk.)

However, if you're installing System 7.1 onto a disk that already has a System file, it's wise to take a few precautions. This applies both to updating an older version of the system and to replacing a System 7.1 installation that you suspect has been corrupted or has become problematical for some other reason.

The Installer will update your existing system. This is perfectly OK most of the time, but to be absolutely safe, especially if you suspect that the system file has become corrupted, you should let the Installer create a new System from scratch. The Installer looks in the system folder for a file named System. If it doesn't find one there, it creates a new one. You can force the Installer to create a new System file by moving the original System file out of the System folder before you launch the Installer.

It's a good idea to rename the old System file so that you can keep track of it. You may want to use it later to retrieve resources such as FKEYs to install them in the new System file.

Wherefore System Enablers?

As we mentioned earlier, one of the benefits of System 7 is its modular nature; new capabilities can be added to it with special system extensions called Enablers, instead of requiring new versions of the system for each new machine. Apple has produced a number of System Enablers for new Mac introduced after System 7.1 arrived.

System 7.1 needs to be "updated" each time Apple releases a new model of the Mac. Back in the days when new Macs only appeared once a year, Apple could and did release new versions of the System to accommodate the new Macs. Now that new Mac models appear every few months, that old way of doing business has obvious drawbacks. Apple's solution is to release a special System 7.1 extension for each new Mac. These special extensions are called Enablers.

Which Enabler Do You Need?

Here's a list of System Enablers, as of April, 1993:

Table 6   *The Names and Version Numbers for the Enablers Required for Various Members of the Mac Line*

Mac	System Enabler Name	Version
Mac Color Classic	System Enabler 401	1.0.4
Mac IIvi	System Enabler 001	1.0.1
Mac IIvx	System Enabler 001	1.0.1
Mac LC III	System Enabler 003	1.0
Mac PowerBook 160	System Enabler 111	1.0.2
Mac PowerBook 180	same	
Mac PowerBook 165c	System Enabler 121	1.0
Mac PowerBook Duo 210	System Enabler 201	1.0.1

Table 6   *The Names and Version Numbers for the Enablers Required for Various Members of the Mac Line (continued)*

Mac	System Enabler Name	Version
Mac PowerBook Duo 230	same	
Mac Quadra 800	System Enabler 040	1.0
Mac Centris 610	same	
Mac Centris 650	same	

If your Mac is listed here (or if it is a later Mac), it *requires* a System Enabler and will not function without it. If your Mac is older than one of these listed, no Enabler is necessary. If you have an Enabler in your System Folder that you don't need, you should delete it.

Apple's numbering convention for Enablers seems decidedly un-Maclike. A naming scheme along the lines of "Mac Quadra Enabler" instead of "System Enabler 040" seems more appropriate, but since the same Enabler file can empower several Mac models, numbering them may be more convenient in the long term.

Installing the System on Macs That Require an Enabler

The set of installation disks for Macs that require an Enabler come with a floppy disk called (in the fine tradition of Lewis Carroll) Install Me First. This disk contains an Installer that supplies the required Enabler. We strongly suggest that you install with this disk first.

Place Enablers in the *Top Level* of the System Folder

The way Enablers function is similar to the way other extensions function. Note that an Enabler must reside in the top or root level of the System Folder. This is unlike standard extensions, which reside in the Extensions folder or Control Panels folder. When you use the Installer, the Enabler is put in its proper place in the System Folder automatically. If you're updating just the Enabler file, drag the icon of the updated Enabler to the icon of the System Folder; the Finder will place it in the top level for you automatically.

What Happens When the Enabler Is Missing?

When Apple says that your Mac requires an Enabler it isn't kidding; your Mac won't boot without it. Instead, you'll get a slightly misleading message that reads "This startup disk will not work on this Macintosh model. Use the latest Installer to update this disk for this model. (System 7.1 does not work on this model; you need a new version that does)." Of course, what you really need is to put the installer back in the top level of the System folder. Boot from the System 7.1 Disk Tools disk for your Mac model and drag the Enabler to the icon of the System folder and restart.

Using MODE32 and 32-Bit Enabler to Break the 8Mb RAM Limit

This tip does not apply to Macs based on the Motorola 68000—the Mac Plus, SE, Classic, and PowerBook 100. Because of the limitations of the early architecture of these Macs, they can address a maximum of 4Mb of RAM.

If you are using a Mac that predates the IIci (that is, the Mac II equipped with optional PMMU, IIx, IIcx the SE/30), then you cannot access more than 8Mb of RAM without special software. The software in the ROMs in these Macs is not "32-bit clean" and cannot deal with larger amounts of RAM.

To access more RAM on these Macs you need a "patch" to the ROM software to make it 32-bit clean. Two such patches are available. Connectix has a product called MODE32, which Apple actually distributed for a while after the release of System 7. Perhaps out of embarrassment, Apple later released its own patch, which it calls the 32-Bit Enabler. MODE32 is by far more reliable and trouble-free, so you should use it rather than the 32-Bit Enabler. Both products can be found wherever Apple System software is distributed.

Extensions and Control Panels and How to Locate Them on Your Hard Disk

Extensions and control panels are small files that actually customize many of the Mac's functions. They are loaded into memory when you boot the Mac. Extensions should be in the Extensions folder in the System folder; Control panels should be in the Control Panels folder in the System folder. Under special circumstances, some extensions are stored in the root directory (top level) of the System Folder.

Order of Extension and Control Panel Loading

Extensions and Control Panels load in this order:

1. The root directory of the System Folder alphabetically

2. Extensions Folder alphabetically

3. Control Panels Folder alphabetically

You can further control the loading order by changing the file's name. To force an extension or control panel to load first, put a space at the beginning of its name.

Choose Your Extensions Conservatively

With the wealth of extensions and control panels available, it's easy to get carried away and install more than you really need, but there are several good reasons to keep the number of them you are using to a minimum:

1. They require memory. If you have many extensions and control panels running, you may find that your System (described in Part 1) has grown to 3Mb or more of RAM. If your system has 20Mb or more, the size of the System Heap isn't an issue. But if you, like many of us, are using a Mac with 8Mb or less of RAM, you'll find that the size and number of the applications you can run is constricted. If your system has only 4Mb of RAM, the size of the System Heap is a constant concern. If your Mac has only 2Mb of RAM, you should be shopping for RAM right now.

2. They slow the Mac down. Many extensions and control panels perform their magic by monitoring everything that's going on in the system and acting accordingly. But if you have too many of them involved in this task, you may find that they are actually slowing your system.

3. They make the machine less reliable. The more programs you have running, particularly extensions and control panels, the greater your chances are for problems to occur. In polite society this phenomenon is called instability.

If You Don't Know Where an Extension Came from or What It Does

Extensions and the magic they do is partly what makes the Mac so much fun, but everything has its price. Many of the problems that get attributed to viruses and other black forces are actually the result of conflicts between extensions. Commercial extensions and control panels (especially versions 2.0 and later) usually work harmoniously. Watch out, however, for noncommercial extensions. The chances of a conflict is much higher with this variety than with commercial ones. See Tip 226.

Why It's Better to Add Extensions One at a Time

Since extensions can conflict and cause your system to be unstable, be very careful when adding new ones to the mix. The best rule of thumb is to add only one at a time. That way, if you start experiencing problems, you'll have a good idea where the source is.

How to Disable All Extensions and Control Panels Temporarily

If you hold down the SHIFT key as your Mac starts up, extensions and control panels that are not required will not launch. Hold the SHIFT key down until the "Welcome to Macintosh" window appears, and the words "Extensions Disabled" appear underneath it. You can then release the SHIFT key.

This disables all nonessential extensions. It does not disable System Enablers (with the exception of the 32-bit enabler), since they are required for your Mac and network and printer extensions. Unless you are intimately familiar with your system extensions, you may be surprised when you start up with no extensions. For example, virtual memory is not activated, and the items in the Startup Items folder are not launched.

Tracking Down Problems with Extensions and Control Panels

Many problems are caused by incompatibilities between various extensions and control panels, the operating system, and application programs. Diagnosing these problems can be a bit tricky.

Use an Extensions Management Utility

The best way to manage conflicts between the extensions and control panels in your system is to use a conflict management utility There are several available. Such a utility—usually control panel—lets you specify which extensions and control panels to load and the order in which to load them.

Extensions Manager, a free offering by Apple's Ricardo Batista, is a bare-bones but capable utility that may provide all the management tool you'll ever need. Most Mac utility packages, such as Now Utilities, also include an extensions manager utility.

1. As a first step, disable *half* the extensions and control panels in your system. If you are not using a startup or extension manager, do this by creating a new folder (the desktop is a good place to put this), and dragging half the extensions and control panels into it. Restart the machine, and see if the problem persists.

2. If the problem goes away, then you know that the problem was probably in one of the extensions or control panels you disabled. Drag half of those you disabled back into the system folder (drag them on top of the closed folder, and the Finder will automatically put them in their proper location).

3. If the problem does persist, then you can remove *half* of those remaining extensions and control panels before restarting.

4. Repeat these steps until you have found the offending extension or control panel.

TIP 230 — Why Not All Extensions Can Get Along

Now, just because you have found it does not necessarily mean this is the sole culprit. Sometimes extensions have conflicts with others that are related solely to the order in which they are loaded when you start your machine. Rename the extension or control panel so that it comes at the beginning or end of the list (use spaces at the beginning of the filename to make it load first; put *z*'s at the beginning of the name to make it load last.). Sometimes this cures the problem. Consult any documentation for the offending control panel to see if it should be loaded before or after any others or if the manufacturer has documented any incompatibilities (these are often found on ReadMe files on the original disks).

TIP 231 — Some Essential Extensions

Even though you should limit the number of extensions in your system folder, there are a few that add what we consider essential to the Mac. Here are some of these categories:

1. *A macro utility, such as QuicKeys or Tempo* If you have an extended keyboard you may have noticed that most of the function keys have no function. You can use Tempo or QuicKeys

to assign functions to them. At the same time, either of these programs can save you a lot of time by coding into them commands that you use often.

2. *A dialog utility* As useful as the Mac's Open and Save dialog boxes are, there is plenty of room for an additional utility. Our favorite is SuperBoomerang (part of the Now Utilities). It remembers the last several locations you visited with open and save dialog boxes and helps you return to them directly the next time you summon the dialog. Once you've used SuperBoomerang, you'll wonder how you ever managed to get anything done on the Mac without it.

3. *Apple extensions, including QuickTime, AppleScript, Macintosh Easy Open* These are all very well-behaved, and add a lot in the way of functionality to your machine.

4. *A file undelete utility* Unlike real life, on the Mac you sometimes regret having just emptied the Trash. There nothing quite like the dull sensation in the pit of your stomach when you realize that you've deleted an important file. Fortunately, if you arm yourself with the proper utility you can undo the unintended file deletion. We've found the undelete function of Norton Utilities and Complete Undelete, part of 911 Utilities from Microcom, to be among the best of the lot.

5. *A virus checker* Although the threat of a virus infection is less than some would have you believe, the threat is real nevertheless. Virus checkers are usually either applications that scan your disk for infection or monitors that scan each disk before it is mounted. The best of the scanners is John Norstaad's Disinfectant. It's freeware and is available from user groups, some dealers, and online services. The best of the disk scanners is Symantec Anti-virus Utilities from Symantec Corporation.

A System Memory Vocabulary

T IP 232

Before you can take maximum advantage of your Mac's memory, you need to develop a working understanding of a few basic terms, specifically the RAM cache, 32-bit addressing, and virtual memory. If these terms are new to you, check the glossary for concise but enlightening definitions of each. Consult Part 1 for tips about specifying memory allocation among the various programs and dealing with memory fragmentation.

One, Two, Many Memory Control Panels

233

General Memory control is handled by the Memory control panel, shown here:

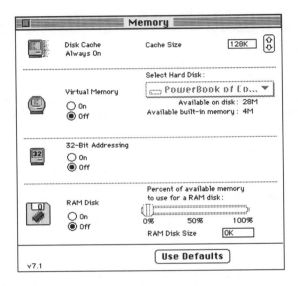

Your Memory control panel might look different from this one. The Virtual Memory option does not appear on 68000 Macs and 68020 Macs (unless you have the optional PMMU or Paged Memory Management Unit for the 68020). The option for enabling 32-bit addressing appears only if your Mac is capable of using 32-bit addressing. The RAM Disk option is for PowerBooks only. In other words, the more options that appear in you Mac's Memory Control Panel, the cooler both you and your Mac are.

Is RAM the Same Thing as Memory?

234

Yes—at least it is in this book.

How Much Memory Can You Install in a Mac?

Older Macs are limited to 4Mb of memory, while new Macs can hold more memory than you're likely to need unless you decide to start a service bureau. To find out how much memory your particular Mac model can address, check with the manual that came with it. Since Apple introduces new Mac models faster than experienced authors can write, we vetoed the idea of including a comprehensive table here. If your manual is missing, or you want to find out the memory capacity of another Mac model, see Tip 236.

"The Mac Memory Guide"

Connectix, developers of Mac memory utilities such as Mode32 and Virtual, publishes a very useful document called "The Mac Memory Guide." It explains how to add RAM to each Mac model. This guide is available as a HyperCard stack or as a printed document. It is available through online services and user groups. You can contact Connectix at 800-950-5880, or at 2655 Campus Drive, San Mateo, CA 94403.

How Much Memory Is Enough

Ideally, you'll probably want to install as much memory as your Mac can handle and your pocketbook will allow.

System 7.1 *requires* 2Mb of RAM just to load. That means that on a 4Mb Mac you have room only to run one medium-sized application or perhaps two small applications. If you use many extensions and control panels and/or need to run larger applications, you'll need 8Mb. If you're the kind of user interested in power and performance, you'll want to install even more memory if your Mac can use it. (Macs have different maximum allowable RAM limits. They also have different restrictions as to which increments of RAM can be added. Consult the manual for your Mac for specifics.)

TIP 238

Disk Cache Settings You Can Live With

You can use the Memory Control Panel Disk Cache setting to set aside a portion of your RAM to hold the data most recently read from disk. The theory is that if the Mac needs that same data again, it can read it from the cache several times faster than reading it from the disk. Even if you know instinctively what the Disk Cache setting in the Memory Control Panel is for, deciding upon the optimum setting is still a mystery.

The general rule is to calculate 32 bytes of RAM for each megabyte of RAM installed. This is also the figure the Memory control panel uses when you click the Use Defaults button. However, there's no real need to set the cache beyond 256K, even if you have more memory. You'll usually get better overall performance if give your applications more of their own memory.

TIP 239

32-bit Addressing: What It Gives You

To use more than 8Mb of physical RAM (and more than 13Mb of virtual memory) you must enable 32-bit addressing. If you don't have more than 8Mb of RAM and aren't using virtual memory, you don't need to use 32-bit addressing, and there's no reason turn it on (though there's no problem with doing so).

The About This Macintosh Display Is a Window to Your Mac's Memory

The Finder's About This Macintosh command (the first item on the Apple menu when the Finder is the frontmost application) gives you some important information about memory usage on your Mac, as well as other facts. Here's what it tells you:

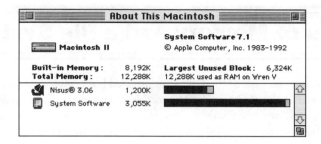

❑ *Mac Model Name* This tells you, if you're curious, which Mac you're using.

❑ *Version and Copyright notice* This tells you the version of the System you are using.

❑ *Built-in Memory* This tells you the amount of physical RAM installed.

❑ *Total memory* This tells you the sum of the built-in memory and the virtual memory you have specified. Divide it by 1024 to translate the figure into Mb. The Total Memory figure is repeated to show you on which disk drive the virtual memory swap file resides.

❑ *Largest Unused Block* This tells you the largest contiguous amount of memory currently available. You cannot run any program that requires more RAM than this amount. This figure may be lower than you expect, which implies that the available memory is fragmented. See Part 1 for more information about fragmented memory.

❑ *Memory Allocation* The lower portion of the window contains a chart showing how much memory is allocated to each running application and how much of that allocation is actually being used.

This last item on this list of running applications is labeled System Software. The memory reserved here is often called the *System Heap* (though technically it encompasses more than the System Heap itself—it also includes memory set aside for the Finder and disk caching). It's the amount of RAM that the Mac needs in addition to RAM needed to run applications. Extensions, control panels, and the disk cache setting all affect the size of the System Heap. If you check the About This Macintosh window from time to time, you'll find that the size of the System Heap varies depending on what the Mac is doing at the time. For example, it grows when a QuickTime movie is playing or an AppleScript script is running, and shrinks when both these activities stop.

TIP 241 Lots of Memory and a Big System Heap

If you have more than 8Mb of memory installed but neglect to turn on 32-bit addressing, the Mac will allocate all the RAM after 8Mb to the System Heap. If you check the About This Macintosh window you'll see a very large System Heap, although the System is actually using only a portion of it. If you have more than 8Mb of RAM, do yourself and your Mac a favor by turning on 32-bit addressing in the Memory Control Panel.

TIP 242 Turning on Virtual Memory

Virtual memory is a scheme in which you instruct the Mac to treat a portion of the hard disk as if it were physical RAM. (Physical RAM is the kind you get when you buy those expensive RAM SIMMs.) You turn on virtual memory with a button in the Memory Control Panel. Virtual memory is not activated until you restart the Mac.

TIP 243 How Virtual Memory Works, and Why You Might Care to Know

This is how virtual memory works. The Mac creates a *swap file* (technically called a "backing store") on the hard disk. This is an invisible file called VM Storage. With virtual memory, physical RAM is swapped to and from the VM disk file as needed to create the illusion that your Mac has more RAM than it really does.

You need to be aware of the size of the VM Storage file. It is equal to the total amount of RAM you specify. For example, if you have 8Mb of physical RAM and use virtual memory to create a total of 16Mb, the resulting disk file is 16Mb. If you have 8Mb of physical RAM and use virtual memory to create an additional 2Mb, the VM disk file is 10Mb.

How to Find Out How Much Virtual Memory You Can Create

Naturally, you can only use virtual memory if you have enough free disk space to create the VM Storage file. The Virtual Memory Control Panel will show you the largest amount of virtual memory you can access.

The Virtual Memory control panel will also tell you if there's not enough free disk space to activate virtual memory.

Turn Off Virtual Memory Before Backing Up Your Hard Disk

Just as you must restart the system after turning on virtual memory to activate it, you must also restart the system after turning off virtual memory in the Control Panel before the space occupied by the VM disk file is freed up. It's much more efficient to turn off Virtual Memory before running your disk backup utility to avoid wasting several Mb of space on your backup medium backing up the otherwise useless VM file.

Virtual Memory is Not a Performance Feature, so Use It Sparingly

As you've probably noticed, your hard disk is not as fast as real memory. You may have noticed reduced performance once the swapping begins. The bottom line is that Virtual Memory is designed to be used only occasionally when your RAM requirements are greater than usual. If you find that you need the extra memory elbow room provide by Virtual Memory on a regular basis, you'll probably decide to invest in more RAM, as Virtual Memory slows system performance noticeably.

Virtual Memory Can Conflict with Some Applications

Some Mac applications use their own schemes for handling virtual memory and conflict with the System's Virtual Memory. Adobe PhotoShop is the most common application in this class. It uses its own virtual memory scheme to allow you to edit much larger photographs than would otherwise fit in available memory. Adobe recommends that you turn off virtual memory when using PhotoShop, and we do, too.

Defragment the Hard Disk for Better Performance

Given that hard disks perform faster when the files are contiguous, Virtual Memory is more efficient if the virtual memory file is not fragmented. See Part 2 for tips on defragmenting your hard disk.

NuBus Slots and How They Affect the Amount of Virtual Memory You Can Create

You can optimize virtual memory by controlling placement of cards in NuBus slots in your Mac. If you have boards installed with empty slots between them, you have, in effect, 1Mb blocks of RAM that are not contiguous with one another (because the Mac allocates a 1Mb address space for each slot). This requires more swapping of memory. The solution is to make sure that all of your NuBus cards are installed next to one another, at one end or the other of the set of NuBus expansion slots. Place the boards at the left edge of the NuBus chain (that is, next to the disk drive, not the power supply). Note that this discussion only applies to the Mac II, IIx, and IIcx, and if you are using Mode32 or the 32-Bit Enabler, it doesn't apply even to those machines.

Use Only Up-to-Date Hard Disk SCSI Drivers

Drivers are small programs on SCSI disks that tell the Mac how to communicate with the disk. Make sure that your hard disk drivers are System 7 compatible. This is particularly true if you are using virtual memory. All disks of which we are aware that were produced since the release of System 7 (in May, 1991) are System 7 compatible, so you only need to worry about this if you are using an older drive.

If you are in doubt about the status of your disk's driver, check with the documentation that came with the drive. Drivers are usually supplied on a utility disk. If you have an Apple hard disk, the drivers are installed on the disk using the HDSetup application.

Third-Party Drivers

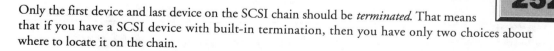

If you are using an older drive with a driver that does not support System 7, or whose company has gone out of business (a not-infrequent occurrence) or the drive manufacturer is not very good at support (also not that infrequent), use one of the third party "universal formatters." The two leaders are Casablanca's Drive7 and FWB's Hard Disk Toolkit. Of the two, we prefer Drive7 for its simplicity of operation and reliability.

Termination

Only the first device and last device on the SCSI chain should be *terminated*. That means that if you have a SCSI device with built-in termination, then you have only two choices about where to locate it on the chain.

If you have but one drive, then that drive should be terminated. Internal drives are always terminated.

How to Use Disk First Aid

253

The first line of defense in scotching hard disk problems is Apple's Disk First Aid. This simple but handy utility is found on the Disk Tools disk that came with System 7. Often Disk First Aid can diagnose and repair simple problems.

Disk First Aid cannot work its magic on the disk from which it is launched. If you have two or more hard disks, you can launch it from a different hard disk. If you only have one disk, launch it from the Disk Tools disk.

Disk First Aid tends to be a bit tight-lipped about what it is up to as it goes about its business of repairing your hard disk. In fact, some things are best left unknown, but if you're strong of constitution, you can press ⌘-tell it to open a window displaying what it is doing.

While Disk First Aid is running, you can press ⌘; this opens up a small window below the main display, showing you what the program is doing.

If Disk First Aid can't fix what's ailing your disk, the next step is to try one of the powerful third-party utilities. The best hard disk utilities are Central Point Software's MacTOOLS and Symantec Corporation's Norton Utilities.

Install a System on Your Second Hard Disk

254

If you have a second hard disk, install System 7 on it. This way, you can boot from it in case of emergency.

Make the Mac Ignore Internal Hard Disk

255

If you have an internal and an external hard disk, you're in much a better position to deal with a problem disk. If you normally boot from the internal disk, and that disk begins causing problems, one workaround is to boot from the external disk if it has a System. Sometimes you can use the Startup Disk Control Panel to select the external disk to tell your Mac to boot from the external drive. But if the problem on the internal drive keeps you from booting from it, you can still force the Mac to boot from the external disk by holding down ⌘-OPTION-SHIFT-BACKSPACE when starting up. This technique requires, of course, that the external disk contains a valid System folder.

How to Start Up from a Bernoulli Cartridge Disk

Bernoulli removable cartridge drives have a quirk that gets in the way of booting from them. They don't spin up until the internal drive itself has started up. The result is that your Mac boots from the internal drive, even if you've specified the Bernoulli cartridge as the startup device. If you use the ⌘-OPTION-SHIFT-BACKSPACE technique described in the previous tip to force the Mac to ignore the internal drive, the Mac behaves as if there were no available boot device, and presents you with the question mark disk icon. Here's how we get around this problem: Specify the Bernoulli as the startup device and then press the programmer's switch to force the Mac to restart. This way, the Bernoulli doesn't spin down, and the Mac boots from it. This emergency technique works even if the Mac won't boot from the internal drive or if it's booted from a floppy disk.

This technique should only be used in an emergency because restarting the Mac by bypassing the proper shutdown procedure is never a good idea.

Mac File Allocation and Lots of Small Files

The Mac stores files more efficiently on Mac volumes that are 32Mb or smaller. Here's why. Files are stored in units called file allocation blocks. The smallest block is 512 bytes. The Mac's limit on the number of file allocation blocks is 65,535 per volume. Math jocks will quickly realize that 512 multiplied by 65,536 is 33,553,920 or 32Mb, for short.

The minimum size of the file allocation block doubles with each multiple of 32Mb, so that the size of the file allocation block on a 500Mb drive is 8Kb. On a drive of this size, a small 4Kb file still occupies the entire 8Kb of disk space.

These calculations are mostly academic unless you deal with hundreds or thousands of very small files of a large volume. In that case, partition the drive to reduce the size of the file allocation block, and thereby increase the number of files you can store on the volume.

TIP 258 Disk Partitioning

You can make one hard disk act like it is actually several by partitioning it. Partitioning a disk effectively creates several SCSI volumes on the same disk. As mentioned in the previous tip, partitioning can be useful, since it actually lets you get more files on disk by letting it work with smaller allocation blocks at a time.

Partitioning can give you a degree of privacy. Most formatting utilities give you the option of assigning a password to a partition. A password-protected volume will not mount at boot time without the proper password.

TIP 259 Hard Disk Partitioning Strategies

A good approach for partitioning is to create one partition for your System Folder. If you are not using virtual memory, then 30Mb should be more than enough to hold the System Folder, if you *are* using virtual memory, add the amount of memory you want to devote to the system partition. If you decide after creating the partition that you want to use virtual memory, but find you haven't left enough room for the necessary swap file, you can use the Memory Control Panel to put the swap file on another drive (or partition).

A second partition might contain your applications. With the size of applications growing, it's difficult to give reliable advice about the size of this partition.

A third partition might contain your data (with the possibility of a fourth, password-protected volume for sensitive data). This approach makes backup a lot more convenient.

Partitioning Lets You Have Two System Folders on the Same Physical Drive

Other than storing large numbers of very small files efficiently, we did find one occasion in which partitioning made life easier. In the course of reviewing several PowerBook utilities, we partitioned the hard disk on a PowerBook. The main partition contained our working environment (system, applications and data). The smaller partition was used for testing purposes only. This allowed us to experiment freely with a variety of utilities, some of which patched the system file, without having to worry about maintaining the pristine purity of our personal PowerBook setup.

Drawbacks to Partitioning a Hard Drive

On the downside of partitioning is the fact that if you don't set your partition sizes wisely, you can end up with a lot of wasted space. For example, you could devote 30Mb to the system partition, only to find that 25Mb would be sufficient. You would then be faced with either ignoring 5Mb of storage capacity or using that space to store applications or documents, which would defeat the reason for partitioning the drive in the first place.

Another down side of dealing with partitions is the fact that it makes opening and saving files a little more complicated as you have to navigate through different volumes. We generally don't partition drives, but we know many wise and experienced users who swear by it.

The End of Computer Virus Denial

Apparently computer viruses will be with us always, although new ones are appearing with decreasing frequency. We think that they pose much less of a threat than some believe, but precautions are still wise. Meanwhile, many Mac anomalies that are attributed to viruses are in fact the result of more mundane factors, including software bugs and system incompatibilities.

Avoiding Viruses

There are several ways to avoid viruses in addition to the virus checking utilities covered in Tip 264.

One good defense is to be aware of how viruses are transmitted. They generally enter your system from an infected file whose recent whereabouts is questionable. This medium might be a floppy or other removable media, or perhaps the file is received via modem from another computer. Examples of systems becoming infected by a virus from freshly opened commercial software are exceedingly rare, although they have occurred.

If you frequent online services and bulletin boards, make sure those services have acceptable anti-virus policies. The sysops of major services such as CompuServe and America Online check uploaded software for viruses before they make it available for others. Make sure that any bulletin boards you use do the same; if they don't, then don't use software from them.

If you get files or software from any other sources, including friends and relatives, make it your policy to check the files for viruses before admitting them to your computer.

Virus Checkers

As we mentioned earlier in Tip 263, a virus checker is an important tool in your Mac survival kit.

Our preferred virus checker is John Norstaad's Disinfectant (at the time of writing the current version is 3.2). Norstaad graciously makes this software available at no charge, and is quick to update it for new viruses when they appear. Like most of the programs we mention, this one can be acquired from user groups, online services, and very helpful dealers. A benefit of Disinfectant is that it watches for activity by *known* viruses; it knows all about the activity of every virus to bite the Mac, and watches only for that activity.

How a Bootable Floppy Disk Can Get You Out of a Jam

TIP 265

Sometimes your only hope of getting your system up and running is to boot from a floppy disk. Any disk utility worth its salt will contain an emergency boot disk that contains a stripped-down System and enough of the utility software itself to get you going. The Disk Tools disk includes a small System. Both the Drive 7 and the MacTools utilities include a disk that contains Enablers for every Mac.

Make Backup Floppies a Part of Your Life

TIP 266

Always make backup copies of the original distribution disk of any software that you use legally. Then use those backups. This may sound like elementary advice, and in a real sense it is, but ignore it at your peril. We know of one regular user who ignored this advice for nearly nine years before the first disk of a critical application installation set became unusable. On the other hand, you have to balance eight-plus years of freedom from the admittedly mundane task of making copies of floppy disks against the day's work that was lost and professionally important deadline that was missed because of the unusable disk. It's your call.

A Bootable Double-Sided (800Kb) Floppy

TIP 267

There are plenty of old Macs, especially Pluses, SE's and Mac II's that use the older double-sided, 800Kb floppy disks. The solution to the problem of creating a bootable floppy drive for these Macs is to create a floppy that contains System 6, preferably System 6.0.5 or System 6.0.8, the two most stable versions of System 6. You can quite easily create a minimal System 6 System that is specific to a particular Mac model and is 800Kb-disk friendly. If you don't have a System 6 disk set hidden away somewhere, check with your dealer or a users group for a free copy. Once you've booted your Mac with this System 6 disk, you can then attempt to perform repairs, such as running HD SetUp, as needed.

Resetting (Zapping) the Parameter RAM (PRAM)

The Mac maintains some system settings in a special kind of RAM, called Parameter RAM or PRAM, so you don't need to constantly set it up over and over again. The settings include date and time, mouse speed, desktop pattern, and others. If you're having trouble with the system, sometimes resetting (often called zapping) PRAM will solve the problem. Here's how.

1. Restart the machine.
2. Hold down the ⌘, OPTION, P, and R keys (all at the same time).

The Mac will begin to boot as normal, and then as it recognizes what you are doing, boot again. When you hear the second system bong sound that signifies the second boot process, you can release the keys.

What's Stored in Parameter RAM (PRAM) and Thus Has to Be Reset when PRAM Is Zapped.

After zapping the PRAM, you'll need to use Control Panel to restore the affected system settings:

❏ *In the General Controls control panel* Reset the Insertion Point blinking speed, Desktop Pattern, and Menu blinking speed.

❏ *In the Mouse Control Panel* Resest the mouse tracking and double-click speeds.

❏ *In Chooser* Reselect the printer and re-enable AppleTalk, if used.

❏ *In the Monitors Control Panel* Reset the color depth.

❑ *In Startup Disk Control Panel* If you have more than one hard disk, the PRAM after zapping resets the disk with the lowest SCSI ID number as the startup disk. If want to specify a different hard disk as the startup disk, set it with the Startup control panel.

Though the PRAM contains the date and time, these don't get reset when the PRAM is zapped.

System Error Alerts When You're in Dire Straits

We were tempted to include a list here of the various alerts the System presents you in the bomb boxes that appear when something has gone seriously wrong. However, such list is not very useful: these are usually catastrophic software errors over which you have little direct control. (By the way, the technical term for this error alert is the DSAT, for Dire Straits Alert Text.) If you find your Mac suffering more than the occasional DSAT, there are some things you can do:

1. If the errors occur in a particular application, try giving that application more memory in which to run (see Part 1 for instructions about this). Well-designed software should be able to deal with low-memory situations, but not all situations can be handled gracefully, and besides, "should" is among the cruelest words.

2. Rebuild the Desktop (as discussed in Part 1). Errors caused by a corrupted desktop file usually occur when you are opening a file or launching an application.

3. Experiment with disabling some Extensions and Control Panels, as discussed in the section covering extensions and control panels.

Contacting Apple's Help Line

As we began to compile the tips in this book Apple announced that it was expanding the toll-free help line established for PowerBook users into a general help system for all in-warranty Mac users. So far it's gotten off to a rocky start, but we're optimistic that with time, it will get better. In fact, we're beginning to receive reports that its service is improving rapidly. The PowerBook support is world class, and there's no reason that the same policies and techniques won't result in world-class support for the rest of Apple's customers. The number is 1-800-SOS-APPL (1-800-707-2775).

Generic Application Tips

This section contains tips that work with all applications or with certain types of applications.

TIP 272 — Read the Manuals

Read the documentation for any software that you use regularly. This is equally true whether you are learning a brand-new program or upgrading to a new version. If you're completely new to a program, you'll probably benefit from following any tutorials that are included. Even if you only expect to use a small subset of a program's features, at least take the time to scan the entire document. This will give you a basic understanding of how the program works, plus you might discover useful features that can make your work time more efficient. The general rule is "Power users read manuals." That's how they become power users.

TIP 273 — Explore the Help System

Acquaint yourself with the program's online help. A scan through the help system can help you find things quickly later and can show you some things you might not have found out about otherwise. The online help is often quite extensive, and using it as a reference is usually much quicker and more convenient than thumbing through the pages of the printed documentation.

TIP 274 — Register Your Software

Almost all software comes with a registration card. Unlike the registration card that came with your toaster or your VCR, sending in the registration card for software has tangible benefits. Registering software usually qualifies you for technical support and almost always qualifies you for relatively inexpensive upgrades to later versions of the software as they become available.

Once you're in the software publisher's database of registered owners, the daily mail can become a bit more interesting. Some manufacturers publish newsletters with tips and answers to support questions about their products, and most send you notices about upgrades. Business practices being what they are, the company that publishes your software will often gleefully sell your name to the junk-mail industry.

Store Registration Numbers and Support Phone Numbers in Your Address File

Whether you keep a paper address book or one in your computer (or both), when you get a new piece of software, enter the vendor of the software into it. If you also add the technical support phone number, the serial number, or the registration number of your software, you'll have that information available any time you have to call for technical support.

When you call for technical support, most vendors ask for your registration number. Although you can sometimes find the registration number in the program's About dialog box, you can avoid this step altogether if you go ahead and enter the registration number in your address book when you enter the phone number for technical support.

Having registration numbers in your address book also makes it easy when you are upgrading to a new version. Sometimes new versions replace old ones when installed on your hard disk, and when you start them up the first time, they ask for the serial number. Again, if it's in your address book, it's easy to find.

Another good location to write the serial number is inside the first page of the manual.

Before Calling Tech Support, Consult the Documentation to Make Sure You Understand the Problem as Well as You Can, and See If You Can Reproduce It

If you need help with a particular aspect of a program, read the manual before calling for technical support. Common problems and their solutions are often detailed in the documentation itself. Since some technical support services require a toll call, and all require a fair amount of time (both waiting on hold and explaining your complex problem), we prefer to solve problems ourselves whenever possible.

If you're calling about a problem with the program, make sure that you can reconstruct the steps that lead to the problem, and read the manual to make sure that you can state it using the terms the program uses for particular steps.

How to Escape from a Frozen Application, Sometimes

Sometimes an application just freezes. The only solution is to restart, which means that in addition to losing any unsaved changes to open documents in that application, you also lose any unsaved changes in documents in all other applications that might also be running. If an application freezes, try the ⌘-OPTION-ESCAPE keyboard combination. It doesn't always work, but when it does, you'll be glad you learned it.

When you escape from a frozen application with this technique, it's very prudent to save all open documents in other applications immediately. Being exceedingly conservative in these matters, we also restart our Macs after saving everything.

How to Avoid the Application Unexpectedly Quit Dialog Box

Although it happens less frequently with System 7.1 than earlier versions of the Mac operating system, your application can quit quite suddenly, presenting only a somewhat cryptic dialog box announcing the obvious. If this happens to us, we check to see that we've allocated enough memory to the application. Usually, granting it more memory greatly reduces the likelihood of the application quitting again.

Use the Automatic Save Feature If It's Available

Many applications include a feature for saving the active document on an interval you determine, either in minutes or number of keystrokes. Given Murphy's Law, it's a good idea to take advantage of this feature. If disaster strikes in the form of an application freeze or a system crash, you will have saved a manageable portion of your work, even if you've been so into your work that you've forgotten about saving it.

Learn the Standard Dialog Box Keyboard Equivalents

Though they are by no means universally implemented, there are some fairly standard keyboard equivalents for dialog box options. We find using keyboard equivalents a lot more convenient than reaching for the mouse, particularly in dialog boxes that we have to deal with frequently. Here's a rundown of some standard keyboard equivalents:

❑ RETURN *and* ENTER *keys* These keys are always synonymous with clicking on the highlighted button. As shown in this Print dialog box, the Print button is highlighted, so pressing either RETURN or ENTER in this dialog box prints the document.

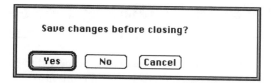

❑ ESC *key* This key usually has the same effect as clicking the Cancel button in a dialog box.

❑ ⌘-. *(period)* This keyboard sequence is sometimes used instead of the ESCAPE Key as an equivalent for clicking the Cancel button in a dialog box.

❑ ⌘-N When you close a document window without having saved first, most applications automatically summon a dialog similar to the one shown here:

In this dialog, the RETURN key will activate the Yes button. The ESCAPE key (or possibly ⌘-.) cancels closing the window. The keyboard equivalent for clicking the No button is usually ⌘-N. Not all applications support keyboard equivalents for Save dialog boxes. Some, including the ubiquitous Microsoft Word, require the N key only, not ⌘-N.

The majority of applications use Yes and No buttons in the Save dialog box. However, Apple's official guidelines for the Mac interface actually specify that software designers use Save and Don't Save, as shown here:

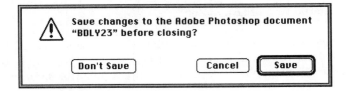

We have found that that applications that ignore popular usage in favor of slavish devotion to the guidelines often have no keyboard equivalents for the Save and Don't Save buttons.

TIP 281 — Explore the OPTION Key

Most applications have many more features than comfortably fit on the average menu. One way that designers implement what some would call "power features" is to use the OPTION key to modify some commands. This technique is often used to bypass dialog boxes. For example, with MacWrite Pro and ClarisWorks, you can bypass the Print dialog box by holding down the OPTION key when you enter the Print command. With CE Software's QuickMail, holding down the OPTION key when you click the Delete message button bypasses the annoying confirmation dialog box. One of the first things we do when evaluating new Mac software is explore how it uses the OPTION key as a modifier.

TIP 282 — Using Paste in Dialog Boxes

Many dialog boxes have fields in which you are expected to enter text—most notably the Save As dialog box. Some applications let you paste text into this field. Generally when a *modal* dialog box appears, the Edit menu is gray and not enabled, so you can't give any of its commands with the mouse. However, you can often use the Edit menu keyboard equivalents for copying (⌘-C) and pasting (⌘-V) text into these fields.

You won't know if the application you're using supports this shortcut until you try it!

Know the Basic Keyboard Shortcuts

That most Mac programs support a basic set of keyboard equivalents for standard operations is a strong contributor to its ease of use. Here's a list of the most commonly used standards:

Operation	Keyboard equivalent
New	⌘-N
Open	⌘-O
Close	⌘-W
Close All	OPTION-⌘-W
Save	⌘-S
Print	⌘-P
Quit	⌘-Q
Undo	⌘-Z
Cut	⌘-X
Copy	⌘-C
Paste	⌘-V
Clear	BACKSPACE/DELETE
Find	⌘-F
Find Again	⌘-G
Select All	⌘-A
Italic	⌘-I
Bold	⌘-B
Underline	⌘-U
Increase point size of selected text	⌘->
Decrease point size of selected text	⌘-<
Extend selection from keyboard	SHIFT-LEFT ARROW or SHIFT-RIGHT ARROW

Make ⌘-S your long-term companion! (See Tip 8.)

Not all of these shortcuts are implemented in all applications. For example, those that do not allow you to format text might use the text formatting shortcuts for other purposes.

Learn the Other Keyboard Shortcuts Your Software Uses

Aside from the basic list of keyboard shortcuts, when learning a new program, it pays off to learn those that are supported by that software. Especially check to see if the standard shortcuts are supported. When we get our hands on a new program we usually check out the keyboard equivalents that we use most frequently to see if they are supported.

What to Do If You Need More Keyboard Equivalents Than Your Application Provides

For those of us who rely heavily on keyboard equivalents, no application really provides enough. If you want more, CE Software's QuicKeys is a godsend. Among its many other features, QuicKeys lets you assign keyboard equivalents to almost any menu command or sequence of menu commands that your application supports.

A Key to Those Strange Menu Symbols

The ⌘ symbol is ancient (in Mac terms) and widely used. When you see it next to a command on a menu along with another character, that means that holding down the ⌘ key and pressing that keyboard character is the same as clicking that command with the mouse. The Mac has two additional modifier keys, called OPTION and CONTROL. In addition, you might encounter symbols for the ENTER, RETURN, BACKSPACE (or DELETE), and INSERT keys. Here's a table of these keys and their symbols:

Symbol	Key Name
⌘	COMMAND
⌥	OPTION
⇧	SHIFT
⌃	CONTROL
↵	RETURN
⌤	ENTER (on the numeric keypad)
␣	SPACE
⇥	TAB
⌫	DELETE or BACKSPACE
▦	Numeric keypad key
⎋	ESC
⌦	DEL (delete forward)
↑,↓,←,→	Arrow keys

Of Files on the Desktop and Desktop Folders

TIP 287

Files you move to the Desktop or save to the Desktop may appear on the Desktop, but behind the scenes, the Finder keeps track of these files by storing them in the Desktop folder in the top level of the volume. This lets the Finder keep track of files on the Desktop, regardless of the volume on which they are actually stored. The Desktop button and the Desktop pop-up refer to the Desktop of the startup volume. In this illustration, Mr. Jones is the name of the startup volume, and it is to that disk's Desktop the file is saved:

If, for some reason, you want to save the file to a desktop folder of a different disk, you can click the name of that disk in the directory listing. Note that the name of the disk at the top right of the dialog box changes when you do so, as shown here, where the disk named 4.syquest has been selected:

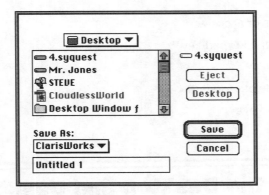

Remember that clicking in the directory portion of the dialog box shifts the focus, so you need to press the TAB key or click on the filename field to move the focus.

Some applications, usually older versions, don't implement this Desktop feature correctly in Open and Save As dialog boxes. The Desktop of another mounted local volume appears in these dialog boxes as Desktop Folder in the top directory for that volume. If you encounter the Desktop Folder in an Open or Save As dialog box and have no network volumes mounted (see Tip 298), it's probably time to update to the current version.

How Applications See the Desktop of Network Volumes

Files on the Desktop of a Mac you are connected to on a network behave differently than files on your local Mac. In the Finder, when you drag a file from a network volume to the Desktop, the Finder presents this dialog box:

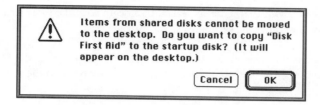

If you click OK, the file is copied to the desktop of your Mac.

Files on the desktop of remote volumes also appear differently in Open and Save As dialog boxes. Rather than in list of desktop items, as described in Tip 287, they appear in the Desktop folder in the top directory of the remote volume. In this illustration, the Desktop folder is in the top level of the remote volume called "Vanagon Valdez."

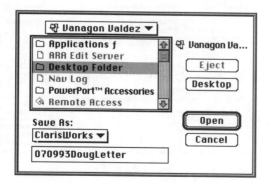

Use Keyboard Equivalents in Open and Save As Dialog Boxes

When you work with Open and Save As dialog boxes, you can use the keyboard in several ways to speed your work.

In the Open dialog box, you can always type the first letter of a file or folder's name to select the first file in the list that begins with that letter. If several files begin with the same letter, you can type the first two or three letters in quick succession to select the file.

The RETURN key opens the selected item; it's synonymous with pressing the Open button. If the selected item is a file, that file is opened in the application you are using. If the selected item is a folder, it opens that folder.

Use ⌘-D to quickly move to the Desktop level in an Open or Save As dialog.

In a Save dialog, when you type a character, it is entered into the field that holds the filename. However, you can move the *focus*—the area to which keystrokes are sent—by using the TAB key. If the focus is in the directory list, then a heavy black line appears around that list, as shown here:

If the focus is on the filename field, you will see either a blinking insertion point or the selected filename. Remember to use the TAB key to move the focus, though you can also move it with the mouse by clicking in either area.

Click on Disk Name in an Open or Save As Dialog Box to Move Up a Folder

When opening or saving a file, you can move up a level in the folder hierarchy by choosing the name of that folder from the pop-up menu above the directory list, as shown here:

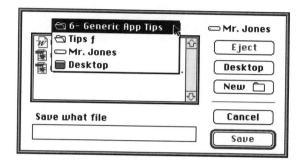

However, there's a shortcut that lets you move *up* a folder in the hierarchy with a single click. You can click on the name of the disk at the right part of the dialog box, and the folder enclosing the current directory becomes the active folder. Successive clicks move you up the hierarchy's successive levels.

Use Standard Extensions for Filenames to Make Them Easier to Find

Though it might seem to be an atavistic holdover from the days when DOS or UNIX were new, it's not a bad idea to append suffixes to filenames to distinguish their use or format.

For example, when working with graphics, you might save them in different formats for different uses. You can then use .pict for the PICT version and .tiff, .eps, and .jpeg for the TIFF, Encapsulated PostScript, and JPEG formats, respectively.

Other standard extensions might include .ltr for a letter and .txt for a text-only version of a file. A happy side effect of this technique is that it makes filenames easier to translate to DOS format, as discussed in Part 4.)

Similarly, when you work on documents that are shared and edited by different users, each user who modifies a file should keep the original filename and append their initials to the end of the filename. For example, in a collaboration between Bob Dylan and Willie Nelson, the first version of the lyric might be stored in file called Heartland.bd. The second version might have the name Heartland.bd.wn, and when Bob Dylan re-edits the lyrics, the file might be called heartland.bd.wn.bd. As you can see, this gives to the filename something of a history of who has edited it.

When the filename reaches more than about 20 characters, the remaining 11 possible characters at the end of the name cannot usually be read in a standard Open dialog box. System 7 then compresses the text of the filename in the dialog box, as shown in the selected file in this Open dialog box:

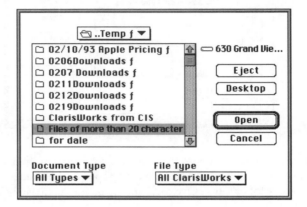

Aliases on the Desktop or in a Desktop Window Folder Make Buried Folders Easy to Find from an Open Dialog Box

One of the reasons we use the Desktop Window folder we discussed in Part 1 is that it makes other folders easy to access. By placing an alias of a commonly-used folder on the desktop, you can easily get to even the most buried folder with just a few clicks. When opening or saving a file, simply click on the Desktop button in the dialog box. You can then either choose the Desktop folder to find your folder's alias, or if you've placed the alias on the desktop, you can get to it directly.

How to Strip Linefeed Characters from Imported Text

When you are importing documents saved as text-only by most DOS-based word processors, you will often find that strange characters appear at the beginning of every line. These are *linefeed characters*— special characters that DOS needs when dealing with text-only files. These characters are usually shown as a box in Mac word processors. There are a couple of ways to get rid of them.

If your word processor allows you to paste text into its Find dialog box, you can select the linefeed character, open the Find dialog box, and paste the linefeed character into the Find field. Next, make sure the field labeled "Replace with" is empty. Then click the Replace All button to replace all the linefeed characters with nothing.

Some word processors also allow you to specify the ASCII code for text you want to find. The linefeed character is ASCII 10 (consult your documentation for instructions on how to use that character).

How to Remove Returns at the End of Every Line

When you retrieve text from online sources, you might encounter files which have a Return character at the end of every line, instead of at the end of every paragraph. Some programs, such as MacWrite Pro and Nisus, have tools that let you automatically remove these line breaks, but if your word processor doesn't have such a tool, here's a tried-and-almost-true recipe for fixing these documents.

1. Make sure that there are *two* returns at the end of every paragraph. If there aren't, manually place the second Return at the end of each paragraph.

2. Use your word processor's Find and Replace function to replace all the cases of two returns with something that doesn't occur elsewhere in the document. We use zzz, but any unique character or characters will do.

3. Use the Find and Replace function to replace each remaining return with a space character.

4. Next, replace all the zzz strings with a return.

We've used this recipe many, many times. The main thing you need to watch out for is cases where there *should* be a return at the end of every line, for example, in a list where each item in the list does not take up the full line. In cases such as these, you can either use the Confirm option of your word processor's Find and Replace feature (instead of Replace All), or select the blocks of text you wish to replace before executing the Replace All command.

Scrolling Through a Document Does Not Change the Location of the Insertion Point

Remember that when you scroll through a document in a word processor (by using the scroll bar or the PGUP or PGDN keys on extended keyboards), the location of the insertion point or selection does not change. That means that you can browse through the document without losing your place.

Returning to the Insertion Point after Scrolling Through a Document

Microsoft Word allows you to return to the selection by typing the 0 key on the numeric keypad (if NUMLOCK is off). Other than that, there is no standard *foolproof* way to scroll the window back to the location of the selection or insertion point. If you've scrolled to another part of the document, the display returns to your selection when you start typing, and any characters you type replace the selection. You can recover the lost selection with the Edit menu's Undo command (⌘-Z).

Summary of Option Keys for Producing Foreign Characters

The Mac supports a number of standard international language characters that you can easily type. Some of them require two keystrokes. To produce any of the characters in the third column, first press the key combination in the first column and then press the key for the letter you want to accent.

Key combination	Produces	Samples
OPTION-`	Grave accent (`)	àèìòù
OPTION-E	Acute accent (´)	áéíóú
OPTION-I	Circumflex, caret (^)	âêîôû
OPTION-N	Tilde (~)	ñ
OPTION-U	Umlaut (¨)	äëïöü
OPTION-C	The letter c with a cedilla	ç

Which Characters Can You Type, and How Do You Do It?

Aside from the standard international characters, the Mac keyboard makes available a number of other characters, which are shown in the following table:

Symbol	Key Combination	Symbol	Key Combination	Symbol	Key Combination
†	OPTION-T	μ	OPTION-M	÷	OPTION-/
°	OPTION-SHIFT-8	∂	OPTION-D	◊	OPTION-SHIFT-V
¢	OPTION-4	Σ	OPTION-W	¤	OPTION-SHIFT-2
£	OPTION-3	Π	OPTION-SHIFT-P	fi	OPTION-SHIFT-5
§	OPTION-6	π	OPTION-P	fl	OPTION-SHIFT-6
•	OPTION-8	∫	OPTION-F	‡	OPTION-SHIFT-7
¶	OPTION-7	ª	OPTION-9	·	OPTION-SHIFT-9
ß	OPTION-S	º	OPTION-0	‰	OPTION-SHIFT-R
®	OPTION-R	Ω	OPTION-Z		OPTION-SHIFT-K
©	OPTION-G	æ	OPTION-'	Œ	OPTION-SHIFT-Q
™	OPTION-2	1	OPTION-SHIFT-B	∪	OPTION-SHIFT-.
Ø	OPTION-O	¿	OPTION-SHIFT-/	œ	OPTION-Q
≠	OPTION-=	¡	OPTION-1	"	OPTION-[
Æ	OPTION-SHIFT-'	¬	OPTION-L	"	OPTION-SHIFT-[
Ø	OPTION-SHIFT-O	√	OPTION-V	«	OPTION-\
∞	OPTION-5	ƒ	OPTION-F	»	OPTION-SHIFT-\
±	OPTION-SHIFT-=	≈	OPTION-X	…	OPTION-;
≤	OPTION-,	Δ	OPTION-J		
≥	OPTION-.	`	OPTION-]		
¥	OPTION-Y	'	OPTION-SHIFT-]		

These characters appear in the TrueType version of Courier as installed when System 7.1 is installed. Many typefaces do not include *all* these characters, and some include characters not shown in the table. Note that the table is literal: If it says to press the SHIFT key, you need to press the SHIFT key—not pressing the SHIFT key generates a different character.

Use Tabs Rather than Spaces to Align Columns of Text

When typing columns of text, make sure that you use your word processor's ruler to set tab stops where you want to align columns, instead of using spaces to make them line up. There are several good reasons for this.

First, it's easier to use tabs than type a number of spaces. Second, unless you use only Courier or another monospaced font, you have the problem of aligning the columns of text with proportionally spaced fonts. Finally, it's much easier to change positions of tabs than it is to realign columns with spaces.

Place Only One Space at the End of a Sentence

Modern design dictates only one space between sentences. If you were trained in the old school and find the old habit of using two spaces hard to break, just use your word processor's find-and-replace feature to replace every occurrence of two spaces with one space.

Place a Bookmark in the Document You Are Working On

Most word processors, ranging from ClarisWorks through Nisus, remember the insertion point when you save a document, so that the next time you open it you're ready to resume work where you left off. Microsoft Word requires an extra step. After you open a document you must press the 0 key on the numeric keypad to scroll the window to the location at which you last did some editing. If your program does not have such a feature, you can insert a character into the file when you close it. We use the β character, which is produced with the OPTION-S combination. This character rarely, if ever, occurs on its own right in our documents, so we aren't likely to be confused by it. By using this character when you open a document you were previously working on, you can simply search for it to find the place where you left off. When it is found, press the BACKSPACE key to delete it, and resume your work.

Save Editions in a Standard Location, in the Project Folder

One of the reasons we recommend organizing your work so that all the files related to a project are kept in the same folder is that it makes those files easier to locate.

This is especially true when you are collaborating on work with others or using Publish and Subscribe to maintain live links between different documents. Placing documents or editions in folders on a server means there is less confusion among users as to where files will be found.

Delete Edition Files When You're Finished with a Project

Editions, the documents produced when you publish a selection of a document, can take up a fair amount of space on disk. This is particularly true of editions that contain graphics information. Since this data is actually contained in three places (in the publishing document, in the edition file, and in the subscribing document), you can save some disk space by deleting editions when the project is finished. If you follow our advice, it's easy to locate editions by using the Finder's Find command.

In the expanded Find dialog box that appears when you click the More Choices button, you can use the Kind pop-up menu to the left to specify that you want to find files of a certain kind. Enter edition in the field to the right to find all the editions. Use the pop-up menu to specify the locations in which the Finder searches.

When Creating a Database, Create Separate Fields for Discrete Units of Information

When creating databases, be sure to isolate items of information from one another for easier formatting and locating of information. For example, in a database to store names and addresses create separate fields for the first and last names. This makes it easier to do other things with the data you have entered, such as sorting it by last name or creating mail-merge letters.

Learn How to Save Tab-Delimited Text Files from Your Database

No matter which database or PIM you are using, you should learn how to make it read and write *tab-delimited files*. Tab-delimited files are those in which fields within a record are separated from one another by Tab characters, and records are separated from one another with Returns. Virtually all databases, spreadsheets, and PIM programs can read and write files in this format. Knowing how your program supports them allows you to transfer data between programs.

Save Templates of Often-Used Documents as Stationery

Whether it's letterhead, a common report format, an envelope format, or a spreadsheet, take advantage of stationery. We explain how to use the Finder to create stationery using the Finder, but some software allows you to save stationery files directly.

The idea is to save settings that you use often, such as margin settings, header information, labeled columns and rows (in a spreadsheet, along with some formulae), letterhead, a return address on an envelope, and more, into a stationery pad. When you retrieve the document, it's often not much more than a fill-in-the-blanks procedure to add specific new information.

Don't Rely Exclusively on Translators

File translators between different word processing formats are a great time saver, but you can't safely depend on them for a completely accurate translation. A translator cannot import features that your word processor doesn't support, and some features, such as tables, almost never survive the transition from one word processor to another intact. Database and spreadsheet translators usually provide only the most basic information, requiring a great deal of reformatting on your part to reconstruct what the translator left out. On the other hand, graphics file translators do a generally very good job.

Avoiding Conflicts Between Your Applications and Fax Software

Most popular fax modem software uses a modifier key to change your application's Print command to a Fax command. If the modifier key conflicts with the application itself, change the modifier to a different key, usually ⌘ or SHIFT. For example, since the OPTION key the GlobalFax fax software included with Global Village modems conflicts with some Claris Corp. applications, we've changed the modifier to ⌘.

Check Your Spelling Checker

Spelling checkers work by comparing words in your document with a built-in dictionary, and are one of the handiest things about computer word processing. However, you still need to proofread your documents, because spelling checkers aren't perfect and don't take into account context when looking at words that have homonyms. For example, in the phrase "Bring that bottle over hear," the word "hear" would not be flagged as a questionable spelling, because "hear" is correctly spelled. Other potential sources of trouble include "there," "their," "its," "it's" "some," "sum," "sun," "son," and similar homonyms.

Grammar Checkers Aren't Worth the Effort

If you can write, grammar checkers don't do anything for you. If you can't write, you'll spend so much time wading through false flags that you still won't gain anything from your considerable efforts. Our advice is to ignore any Mac grammar checker you encounter.

Compose Documents in a Font You Find Readable and Do All the Fancy Formatting Last

Sometimes a finished document needs to be printed in a small font or one that looks better at the higher resolution of a laser printer than it does on the screen. In that case, use a font that you find more readable (we can recommend either Courier—though many people hate Courier—or the Boston font, which is very legible and useful on PowerBooks equipped with passive matrix screens, such as the 140, 145, and 160).

If you use word processors that support style sheets, such as Microsoft Word, MacWrite Pro, PageMaker, or Nisus, you can create separate style sheet documents for editing and for final printing.

If You Have Vision Problems, Use an Application That Supports a Magnified View.

Some programs, including MacWrite Pro, ClarisWorks, FileMaker Pro, let you work in a magnified view of the screen. Though primarily designed to let you make minute changes to a document, this magnified view is also useful for those with vision problems.

Another solution is to do most of your creative work using a large font or set of fonts, and then change the document to a smaller font for final printing. As with Tip 311, this is very useful if you are using a program that supports style sheets.

Choosing Applications to Use on a PowerBook

Unless your PowerBook has a very large hard disk and more than a few megabytes of RAM (memory), you might find that it can't easily handle all the applications you want to use on it and all of your documents. One very workable solution is to use a capable integrated application to replace all but your primary application. An integrated application includes word processor, database, spreadsheet, graphics and communications capabilities in a inexpensive, tidy package. Or favorite is ClarisWorks because of its useful suite of capabilities and its very usable integration. Unless you're dealing with large graphics, it runs comfortably in a 900Kb of memory and occupies only 602Kb on disk, not counting dictionaries and file translators. It can read and write most common file formats. We use Nisus as our primary application and rely on ClarisWorks for most other needs.

For PowerBook word processing Microsoft Word 5.1 has a special PowerBook installation option that consumes much less disk space and battery charge than the standard install. Nisus Corp. offers Nisus Compact, and WordPerfect Corp. offers LetterPerfect for those needing a more manageable version of their mainstream products.

PART

7

Healthy Computing

Over the last few years, the amount of attention that's been paid to various forms of *Repetitive Stress Injuries* (RSI), which includes such things as Carpal Tunnel Syndrome, Tendinitis, Tenosynovitis, Thoracic Outlet Syndrome, and others, has increased, along with the number of sufferers from these injuries. And one of the authors of this book has suffered himself from tendinitis.

The tips in this chapter are *not* just for readers who have already suffered. We hope that serious computer users will take them to heart as tips for *avoiding* problems that can occur among all who use computers for many hours of most every day.

The reason we get these injuries is simply because the human body wasn't designed to sit and do the same thing hour after hour, day after day. Keeping that in mind while working is the best way to minimize the chances of injury.

We Are Not Doctors and Don't Play Them on TV

While we gathered the tips for this chapter from a variety of sources, we are *not* doctors. Don't follow any of our tips instead of following what your doctor tells you. And if you are suffering from any sort of pain related to your work, do *not* use these tips in lieu of a trip to your doctor.

What Kinds of Problems Can Unhealthy Computing Lead To?

Though Carpal Tunnnel Syndrome is the most widely-known RSI ailment, there are a number of others. The following are some of the common ones.

Carpal Tunnel Syndrome (CTS)

This nearly debilitating wrist disease is caused by inflamation in the carpal tunnel in the wrist. In this area, nine tendons (for controlling the wrist and fingers), the median nerve (which gives sensation and movement to the fingers), an artery, and a vein pass from the forearm to the wrist. When you move your wrist, the tendons slide back and forth inside this tunnel. Then, if you bend your wrist while moving your fingers (as when typing), the tendons pull through at an angle, rubbing against one another. There, as they say, is the rub; too much of this kind of movement irritates the tendons, swelling them. As they swell, they press against the median nerve, causing pain.

Symptoms of CTS include a burning or tingling sensation in the first three fingers of the hand, numbness, and pain at night. The pain at night comes from the body retaining more fluids, causing increased pressure on the median nerve. The pain may extend farther, up the forearm to the elbow and shoulder.

Aside from many of the specific tips in this chapter, the best way to avoid CTS is to make sure the wrist is held in a "neutral" position as you type. A neutral position is when the wrist extends in a straight line from the forearm, and is not bent.

CTS sufferers will often need to wear braces on their wrists and lower forearms to help them keep their wrists straight. It's important that CTS be caught early, so that these milder treatments can have an effect. Left untreated too long, CTS may require injections of steroids and surgery.

Tendinitis

Tendons are the connective tissue that anchor muscles to bone. When overworked, the tendons that control the fingers (which are anchored at the elbow) can detach from the bone, swell, or become scarred. This is *tendinitis*, and you've probably read about it in the sports pages, as it often affects athletes.

The related *Tenosynovitis* happens when the membrane sheaths which contain the tendons becomes inflamed. Normally, these sheaths contain a small amount of fluid to provide lubrication. When infected, these sheaths accumulate fluid, causing swelling and pain. The sheaths can be injected with cortizone or drained. Anti-inflammatory drugs, such as Ibuprophin, can reduce the amount of fluid.

Lower Back Pain

Lower back pain is, well, pain in the lower back. The best prevention for it, as with the other repetitive stress injuries mentioned in this section, is a good workspace.

Vision Problems

Vision problems are rare, but they can happen when you spend long hours staring at a computer monitor at a fixed distance from your eyes. After many such long hours, you might notice that it is hard to focus on objects that are nearer or farther from you than the monitor. The best way to prevent this is to keep your eyeballs exercised by periodically focusing on things farther away from the screen, if only for a few minutes every hour or so.

At the First Sign of Trouble, Knock Off Work

If you are experiencing any pain that seems as if it might be connected to your work at the computer, don't try to "work through the pain;"— *it can't be done.* Early signs of trouble include tingling in the wrists, the backs of the hands, and the fingers, pain in your fingers, wrists, or forearms, and pain in the lower back. At the first sign of any of these problems, stop working for at least several hours. Before returning to work, take special care to examine your work space to make sure your posture is correct and that your wrists and arms are positioned correctly.

Make Sure Your Doctor Understands Your Problem

Though various forms of RSI are becoming more and more common, not all general practitioners have experience or expertise with the problem. On your first visit to your doctor, ask if he or she is experienced, and if not, ask for a referral to another doctor who is.

Some problems, such as the various forms of tendinitis, are common to other occupations, such as sports. Some forms of tendinitis are also known as "golfers' or tennis elbow." Many have found that *sports* doctors are good at treating this.

The RSI Network Newsletters Are a Great Source of Information

Caroline Rose publishes an electronic newsletter for RSI sufferers, called *The RSI Network Newsletter.* This newsletter is edited and distributed electroincally by Craig O'Donnell, so a text file of the newsletter is now available in many online services, such as the Internet, BMUG's and BCS's bulletin board systems, the ZiffNet's Download/Technical Support forum on CompuServe. Rose is an RSI sufferer, and because of this, only publishes quarterly. However, even older issues have a lot of good information in them. While we gathered many tips for this chapter from her newsletters, there is a lot information (such as recommendations for physicians and product reviews) that we did not incorporate. All sufferers from some type of RSI should take a good look at the *RSI Network* newsletters.

Those interested in subscribing to future issues can send e-mail to the Internet account <dadadata@world.std.com>. Just type **RSI Subscription** in the Subject: line; No message is required.

Avoid Using Stiff Squeeze Bottles, and Use Larger Padded Handles on Tools

When you are suffering from CTS or tendinitis, avoid using items, such as shampoo bottles, that are stiff and require extra effort to squeeze. If necessary, drain the contents of those bottles into bottles from which you can pour or that are easier to squeeze.

By the same token, avoid using tools (such as pliers, screwdrivers, etc.) that require a lot of pressure to use. Try to find tools (such as screwdrivers) that have larger handles, so you don't have to squeeze your hand so hard.

Warm Yourself Up before Working, Don't Work When Cold

You know the feeling: starting work on a cold winter morning when your fingers are stiff and can hardly move. Don't work at those times until you have warmed yourself up, perhaps, using the limbering exercises listed in the next tip.

You can also warm up in the shower or wear gloves for a few minutes before gradually easing into your work.

Limbering Exercises for the Fingers and Wrists

The following illustration shows some limbering exercises for the fingers and wrists. We find these exercises to be useful on cold mornings or at other times when our fingers are stiff:

LIMBERING UP EXERCISES

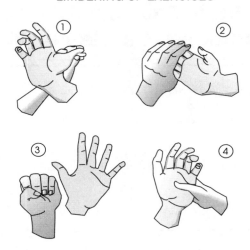

1. To begin, slowly pull your thumb back until you feel it stretch. Hold it back for 5 seconds.

2. Then, holding your other fingers, slowly bend back your wrist and hold it for 5 seconds.

3. Next, make a tight fist and release, spreading the fingers as much as possible. Do this 5 times.

4. Finally, massage your hand back and front, as shown here.

Another good limbering technique is to lightly squeeze a ball, such as a tennis ball, until your fingers are warmed.

Take Breaks Every Hour

When engaged in long sessions at the keyboard, take breaks every hour or so. *Don't* take the break at the keyboard. Stand up, stretch, and walk around a little. Life as we know it extends well past the confines of your desk.

Take Shorter Breaks Every 10 Minutes or So

Even while you are working (between breaks, as it were), take a break from the keyboard every ten minutes or so, especially when you are doing a lot of serious typing and mousing. Move your hands from the keyboard, roll your chair back, and hang your hands at your sides, fingers resting neutrally. Move your vision from the computer screen, and focus on something farther away.

Vary Your Tasks Through the Day

It's hard to do in a lot of situations, but try not to spend all day typing and using your mouse. If you have other, non-computer related tasks, try to intersperse them with your desk work.

Move Your Eyes from the Screen and Look at Things Faraway Periodically

When you're taking your break, try to look at things that are faraway. This gives the focusing mechanisms of your eyes some exercise.

Use a Chair at the Right Height, with Lower Back Support

Given the amount of time you spend in it while working, make sure that you use a chair that helps place your body at the proper angles. Good chairs are expensive, but their cost is nearly nothing compared to the costs associated with a medical problem caused by the wrong chair. To have your employer pay for one will almost certainly involve a note from your doctor or a sports medicine specialist explaining that you must have a fully adjustable chair of your choice. Why "of your choice?" Because no two people are alike, and the chair you select needs to fit you as perfectly as possible. Prices for fully adjustable chairs run from about $500 to over $1000, with $700 or so an average price for a simple chair (no leather, no extras).

❏ *Height* The seat of the chair should be at a level that allows your feet to rest squarely on the floor, with your thighs at a 90 degree angle from your back, and with your knees bent at a 90 degree angle.

❏ *Back Rest* The back rest should fit the curve of the lower back, providing support for it and encouraging you to sit straight.

❏ *Seat* The seat of the chair should incline forward a bit to shift pressure from your lower back to your thighs and feet, so they are helping hold you in place.

Place the Monitor at the Correct Distance and Angles from Your Eyes

The monitor should be at arms' length (15" to 32") from your eyes.

The top of the monitor should be at approximate eye level when looking straight; the bottom of the monitor should then be about 15 degrees below eye level.

This is more difficult when using very large monitors because you have to move the monitor back farther.

Use a Document Holder next to the Monitor at Screen Height

If you spend time referring to or copying from printed documents, then make sure you use a document holder that is mounted next to the screen (or attached to it). It should be at the same height, angle, and distance mentioned in the previous tip, and as close to the monitor as possible.

Follow the Rule of Right Angles for Comfortable Typing

When typing follow the rule of right angles: your forearms should be at right angles to your upper arms, which should be hanging straight down from your shoulders. Your thighs should be at right angles to your torso, and the knees should be bent at right angles.

Have Ample Legroom under Your Desk to Allow Stretching

Don't pile a lot of stuff under your desk that prevents you from moving your feet around. Keep your feet resting flat on the floor while typing, but during short breaks stretch your legs.

Keep Those Wrists Straight

Keep your wrists sraight while typing. A major cause of CTS and tendinitis is typing with your wrists bent (either downward or upward; both are equally bad). Your wrists should extend straight from your forearm, at the same angle formed when hanging your arms freely at your sides (no angle at all).

Since keyboards are higher than the desks on which they rest, this presents a problem; you don't want to expend a lot of energy holding your arms high enough to keep this angle neutral.

Wrist pads are available, made out of foam, that sit in front of the keyboard and provide a resting place for the wrists. These pads are inexpensive, and are one of the best investments you can make in wrist health. The wrist rest should be at the same level as the "home row" on your keyboard. Use a flat wrist rest, and actually, rest the heels of your hand on it, not your wrists.

Don't Hold Your Fingers in the Typing Position When You're Not Typing

When you're not typing, don't hold your fingers in typing position. Even if it's for just a moment's reflection, searching for "le mot juste," take your hands from the keyboard and hang them down at your sides.

Don't Grip the Mouse Too Hard

Try to use the mouse by letting your hand rest on it, grasping it just firm enough to maintain control of it with your fingers in as neutral a position as possible.

The mouse Apple shipped with the Mac until early 1993 was really too narrow; it almost *required* that you grasp it firmly. The new mouse Apple began shipping in early 1993 is somewhat fatter, requiring less of a firm grip. If you are having problems and suspect they are mouse related, upgrade to a newer mouse or use the MouseTopper product mentioned later in Tip 339.

Try Using the Mouse with Your Other Hand

If your wrists, elbows, or fingers hurt when using the mouse with your favored hand, try using it with the other hand. Depending on your degree of ambidexterity (and who wouldn't give their right arm to be ambidextrous), this may or may not be a reasonable option. Though resolutely right-handed, we have developed a degree of mouse ambidexterity after some practice.

Use Utility Software to Help Keep Typing and Mouse Use to a Minimum

Many utilities can help you by letting you perform many actions with a single mouse click or keystroke.

❑ *QuicKeys and Tempo* These two utilities, which we have mentioned elsewhere, let you record sequences of keystrokes and mouse movements, and trigger them with a single keystroke. We find them useful for two reasons. First, by performing long tasks they help relieve some strain. An example is typing your name and address at the top of a letter. If you assign this to a macro, then that's just that many fewer keystrokes you have to type (saving letterhead as stationery can also help). Second, long macros can take a few moments to run, giving you a chance to relax and take a short rest.

❑ *Easy Access* See Part 2 for details on using Easy Access, system software provided with every Mac. Easy Access is of limited use for preventing injuries, but it's a great help if you are suffering from RSI pain.

Use Alternate Input Devices

If you're experiencing pain using your mouse and keyboard, there are plenty of alternate input devices available.

The most common alternate input devices are *trackballs*. Controlling a trackball requires a different set of motions (and thus a different set of muscles) than using a mouse. Some trackballs are designed to be "ergonomic" and feature larger balls and/or rests for your wrists. Be sure to try one before you purchase any of them, or try to get a return guarantee if the trackball is not helpful to you. Since no two people are alike, for example, what's perfect for Ms. Blake can be completely unsuited for Ms. Morris. You might have to try several different trackballs to find the one that's best for you.

There is even one trackball, made by Curtis, which has a separate switch (or button) that can be controlled *by your foot*. This means that your index finger won't tire as you use it, but you will need to be careful about what music you're listening to when your foot is poised above the mouse.

Other Software Designed to Help Prevent RSI

Other software is available that can help you in several ways. There are a couple of programs that bring up dialog boxes on the screen to remind you to take breaks. You can set the intervals at which they appear. An example of this is Visionary Software's LifeGuard.

Another class of software gives the computer "*clairvoyance*," the ability to predict what a word or a phrase will be based on its first few keystrokes. Examples include Berkeley Systems' ScreenKeys, Tactic Software's Magic Typist, and McIntyre Computer Systems' WordWriter. Our experience with these programs is limited. When well-implemented, they can help you type fewer keystrokes.

Apple's Adjustable Keyboard

In January 1993, Apple introduced a *"split" keyboard*. This keyboard is in two pieces and is tilted. You can adjust the angle at which the two pieces meet, letting you type with your fingers and wrists at a more neutral position than they are when using the standard keyboard. (Apple's keyboard resembles somewhat a keyboard called the "Tony" keyboard, which was designed for ergonomics, but so far has not been produced. The Tony keyboard was designed to adjust vertically as well, giving you more control over the angle of your wrists.)

Apple's keyboard has a list price of about $219, compared to $179 or so for the standard extended keyboard.

Reaction to Apple's keyboard among those who have used it has been mixed for several reasons. First, Apple placed the function keys on a keypad separate from the main keyboard, making them harder to reach. Second, the keys on this separate keyboard are much smaller than traditional keys and require more force to press. Finally, the split keyboard requires more desk space than the exended keyboard.

We recommend that you examine this keyboard and test it carefully before purchasing it. If possible, get a return agreement.

Mouse Topper

TIP 339

Contour Systems' *Mouse Topper* is a replacement for the top half of your older Apple mouse. It's much larger than that mouse, making for a more relaxed grip, and is inexpensive and easy to install.

New Apple Mouse

TIP 340

The latest version of the standard Macintosh mouse is called the *Apple Desktop Bus Mouse II*. It is somewhat wider than the previous mouse, meaning that it fits more naturally in the hand, allowing you to use it without requiring you to actually grasp it tightly. It is currently shipping with all Macs, and you can purchase it separately for about $79.

Reducing Screen Glare

TIP 341

Glare on your monitor surface can lead to poor posture as you twist your body to avoid the glare. To avoid glare, position the monitor so that it's not facing a window (this may require moving your desk as well).

Another way to avoid glare is to purchase an *anti-glare screen* for your monitor. Kensington Microware makes a line of anti-glare screens for most Macintosh monitors, at prices ranging from about $50 for the Mac Plus or SE models to $200 for those that fit Radius 21 inch monitors. Polaroid also has a line of circular polarizing filters, priced in the same range. However, some anti-glare screens dim the screen too much, so try to get a return option as part of your agreement to purchase the screen, so that you can return it if it doesn't work for you.

PART 8

PowerBook Tips

While the PowerBook offers 99 percent of the functionality of a desktop Mac, some compromises were made along the way. This chapter offers tips specifically tailored to help you get the most out of your PowerBook. There are more PowerBook models than you might care to learn about. They can be divided into three categories: the discontinued 100, all other PowerBook models from the 140 through the 185c (referred to here as 100-series PowerBooks), and the Duos. Except where noted, all tips apply to all PowerBook models.

Maximum Performance or Maximum Conservation?

The key to getting the most time from a battery charge is to minimize those activities that consume the most power. This means a few compromises in performance; the more compromises you're willing to make the longer your battery will last without needing recharging. The two largest power consumers are the CPU and the backlit screen. They are controlled by two System 7.1 control panels: PowerBook for the CPU and PowerBook Display for the screen.

Slow the Processor to Extend Battery Charge

There are two ways of reducing the power required by the CPU and both are controlled by the System 7 PowerBook desk accessory. *Processor cycling* is the name used for the technique of resting the CPU during periods of inactivity. A resting CPU requires much less power. Processor Speed is an option for all PowerBooks running at 25MHz clock speed or faster. When enabled, it reduces the processor speed to 16MHz. The slower the processing speed, the less power required. Both of these features are accessible via the PowerBook control panel when you click the option button. When you need maximum battery charge life, check the Allow cycling and Reduce speed buttons.

Dim Backlighting to Extend Battery Charge

The backlighting for the PowerBook display is, along with the CPU, the biggest power consumer. The System 7.1 PowerBook Display control panel has a slider control to set the minutes (1 to 5) of inactivity before the backlighting is turned off and the screen is dimmed. Since a dimmed screen comes to life instantly when a key is pressed or the trackball is moved, you might find that setting the slider to one minute before dimming is an easy compromise to make for the sake of prolonged battery life.

Sleep as an Energy Conservation Technique

There are two kinds of sleep, both of which are controlled by the Battery Conservation slider control in the System 7.1 PowerBook control panel. Hard disk sleep refers to the technique of spinning down the disk platter to conserve power. System sleep conserves power by both spinning down the hard drive and dimming the screen. When you set the slider control to Maximum Performance, the system sleeps after about 15 minutes of inactivity. When you set the slider control to Maximum Conservation, system sleep is invoked after a minute of inactivity.

How to Overcome Compulsive Battery Watching

The PowerBook battery charge never lasts long enough. As a result, charge conservation techniques have become somewhat of a fetish among some users. They need more control over power consumption than System 7.1's somewhat anemic tools provide, so they turn to one of the commercial PowerBook utilities, which let you tweak power consumption to your heart's content. These utilities provide a variety of features in addition to power saving, and you really can't take maximum advantage of a PowerBook without one of them (See Tips 352 and 372). Nevertheless, we find compulsive power monitoring much less rewarding than actually getting work done. As a result, the best way to deal with short battery charge is to get more battery power, either by purchasing additional PowerBook batteries or by using a longer lasting external battery, as described in Tips 347 and 348.

TIP 347 · Our Favorite External Battery

We think life is too short and work is too much like work to expend more than a minimum amount of mental energy worrying about batteries. So whenever we know that we'll be needing to run a PowerBook without the benefits of AC power for more than three or four hours, we use an external battery supply. These recommendations apply to 100-series PowerBooks, not to Duos. Our favorite is the VST ThinPack. It weighs just 20 ounces and is about the size of a half-inch thick paperback book, so it easily fits into almost any existing PowerBook carrying case. Under normal conditions it lasts from five to eight hours. (We've been on longer flights, but we've never been willing to work much longer than that while in the air.)

TIP 348 · The Lightest Possible External Battery

If you occasionally only need the extended battery life that you get from external batteries, Lind Electronic Design has a good solution that is available in two models, one for 100-series PowerBooks (APP-3) and one for Duos (APP-5). It's actually a case that holds eight D-cell batteries, and it will last for six to eight hours under normal conditions. Although it's a bit bulkier than the ThinPack described in Tip 347, it's very light (only a few ounces) when empty. That means you can avoid lugging around a fair amount of otherwise dead weight; you can purchase batteries just before you board a plane, for example, and dispose of them after you get off.

TIP 349 · The Car Cigarette Lighter Charger Solution

Here's a way to make all that time you may be spending behind the wheel of your car a bit more productive. With the proper adapter for your car cigarette lighter, you can charge your PowerBook as you drive. We use the one made by Lind Electronic Design (model PB-1 Auto Adapter). If you're comfortable with alligator clips, you can install a lighter receptacle (available at most auto supply stores) in the trunk. This setup lets you charge the PowerBook battery with only a little more bother than putting the PowerBook in your trunk.

How to Swap Batteries Without Shutting Down First

If you travel with your PowerBook, one of your first accessory purchases will probably be a second battery pack. But shutting down your 100-series PowerBook to swap out the old battery for the new one is a time and power-consuming bother. The solution is the Utilitron PowerSwap. It's a small external battery (standard 9-volt) that can power your PowerBook long enough for you to swap the internal battery pack.

The Advantages of a Second AC Adapter

If you regularly use your PowerBook at two or more offices (or between home and an office), there are several advantages to purchasing a second AC adapter. You avoid the hassle and weight of toting an adapter between the two locations. You also free yourself from worrying about battery charge at the second location. As new 100-series models were introduced, Apple increased the wattage of PowerBook AC adapters. These more-powerful adapters work with older PowerBooks, and since they charge batteries faster, be sure you don't buy an older one that has been sitting in your dealer's storeroom. Look for a model marked 24W (model M5652). Higher wattage models may be available as you read this. If you don't plan to use your AC adapter outside the US., consider the Kensington PowerBook AC Adapter. This 100-series adapter is smaller and lighter than Apple's, but it's rated at 120 volts only, so it's not appropriate for the intercontinental traveler.

Picking a PowerBook Utility

There's a booming market in utilities designed to overcome some of the shortcomings of the PowerBook. At press time even Apple was getting into the act with its own offering. These utilities offer extensive control over power consumption, more sleep options, password security, AppleTalk behavior, and keyboard equivalents for extended keyboard keys missing from the PowerBook keyboard. Dale has reviewed all of these products for MacWEEK, and two clearly stand out from the pack: CPU 2.0 (Connectix PowerBook Utilities) from Connectix Corp., and Billy Steinberg's PBTools from Inline Design. CPU 2.0 offers more features than any one user is likely to need, including customizable settings for different individuals, different applications, different operating environments, a really slick brightness slider control, and file synchronization. The best of the litter, however, is PBTools. It's a model of intelligent, clean design, and does the best job of monitoring remaining battery charge. It is also a single control panel and uses the least amount of precious PowerBook RAM.

What to Use for Deferred Printing and Faxing

Sometimes when you're on the road with your PowerBook, you might find that you're ready to print or fax a document, even though there's no printer or phone line at hand. If this situation annoys you, Palomar Software's On the Road utility is the answer. It lets you go ahead and issue the print and fax commands when you want, saves the output as a file on disk, then sends it along automatically when you reconnect to a network.

Battery Care (What You Need to Know About Discharge)

How you care for your PowerBook batteries depends on which kind of PowerBook you use:

❏ *PowerBook 100* This now discontinued PowerBook uses lead/acid batteries. Never completely discharge a PowerBook 100 battery purposely. Reconnect the AC adapter as soon as you receive the alert dialog stating that no charge remains.

❏ *100-series* These PowerBooks use NiCad (Nickel/Cadmium) batteries. NiCad batteries should be completely discharged about once every month or two to avoid the "memory effect," a condition theoretically caused by charging the battery incompletely. This is a controversial subject that has divided the PowerBook community into believers and non-believers. We don't know which camp holds the truth, but we periodically discharge our NiCad batteries anyway, either by letting the PowerBook run until after the last alert or with a Lind Electronic Design external charger. So far, we've never encountered the memory effect, and nothing bad has happened to our NiCad batteries, either.

❏ *Duos* The more modern PowerBooks use NiHy (Nickel/Metal Hydride) batteries. They aren't subject to the memory effect, at least in theory, although Apple says to recondition them periodically by discharging them. Unlike NiCad batteries, NiHy batteries tend to lose their charge when stored for long periods.

Charge Your Batteries Fully

The NiCad batteries in 100-series PowerBooks charge in two steps, called fast charge and trickle mode. A discharged battery reaches about 80 percent of its capacity within two hours (fast charge). After that, it converts to trickle mode, which takes about four more hours to reach the maximum charge. The Battery DA usually reports that the battery is fully charged when it finishes fast charge mode. To get a complete charge, let the battery charge for six full hours.

Use Extensions Judiciously When Memory Is in Short Supply

Apple has never been particularly generous when deciding on minimum configurations for its products. All PowerBooks ship with only 4Mb of RAM; you have to purchase additional memory either from Apple (never a cost-effective course of action) or a reputable third-party vendor. If you're using this minimum-RAM configuration, you can make more memory available for running applications by reducing the amount of memory required by the System itself. One of the easiest ways to do this is to reduce the number of extensions to a minimum. Load only those that you absolutely need. Perhaps by the time you get tired of making this sort of compromise you'll be more inclined to purchase additional RAM. When you do so, get as much as your PowerBook will support and that you can reasonably afford. For many users, upgrading to 8Mb of total RAM gives your applications all the breathing room they need, with the added advantage of letting you load a large number of extensions freely.

Adjust Application Memory Allocations Downward with Care

One good way to work in an environment in which memory is in short supply is to lower the memory allocation with the Get Info command. The tradeoff with this strategy is that the application might run slower. Some applications, such as ClarisWorks, load the entire document into memory. With these applications, lowering the memory allocation reduces the size and number of documents that you can load. If you find that an application repeatedly quits on its own (usually accompanied with the "quit unexpectedly Type 1 error" dialog), you should allocate it more memory.

Lowering the memory allocation of some applications (such as Microsoft Word, or FileMaker Pro) also means that the application does not have as much RAM for documents as it might like. These applications can work with less RAM, but will consequently need to read from the disk more often, thus shortening battery life.

Leave the System Some Breathing Room

When working on a 4Mb PowerBook, it's tempting to adjust application memory sizes to the minimum so you can get just one more application loaded. This strategy works for many users, although minimum application memory allocations make some applications run slower and limit the number and size of open documents in those that load documents entirely in memory. Bear in mind, however, that the System itself needs additional RAM from time to time. Running several applications can increase the System heap, and some desk accessories use more memory than the 20K allocated to them by the Finder.

Repartition Your Drive to Recover Hidden Capacity

As it is shipped from the factory, your PowerBook internal disk drive has some additional space that Apple has chosen not to make available to you. That's because although Apple drives are available in standard sizes (40, 80 and 120Mb), the drives provided by the manufacturers from which Apple purchases the drives are of slightly varying sizes. Apple rounds down to these standard capacities to make life simpler for both those selling and those buying its products. You can use the Apple HD SC Setup utility on the Disk Tools disk to repartition the drive to recover this wasted space. Dale used this technique to recover 1.6Mb of space on his PowerBook 140 40Mb drive; other users have reported recovering up to 7 or 8Mb of wasted space on larger drives.

Memory Upgrades

Not all PowerBook SIMMs are created equal. Buy from major vendors to be safe. That doesn't mean you have to pay Apple's usually inflated prices. Approved vendors include Microtech, Newer Technology and some others. Unless you have experience exposing the guts of computers, it's worth paying a reasonable premium (around 20 percent) to purchase and install the SIMMs from a reputable, authorized dealer. In addition to avoiding the hassle of performing the task yourself, if something goes wrong, it's the dealer's responsibility, and you keep any warranty you have remaining on your PowerBook intact.

Selecting a PowerBook for External Video

The first-generation PowerBooks (100, 140, and 170) did not include the circuitry to drive a standard display. The 160, 165c, 180 and 180c do include this feature. If you need to use an external display with your PowerBook, you'll be better off purchasing one of the later PowerBooks that includes this feature. The third-party products that add this feature to earlier PowerBooks are less than completely satisfactory.

Connecting a VGA or Multisync Monitor to a PowerBook

If you think you will need to connect a VGA or multisync monitor to your PowerBook, investigate Apple's PowerBook PC Companion. It includes a special adapter called the MacVGA for this purpose.

Do You Need to Take a Printer with You?

Most users find that they can function quite well with their PowerBook on the road without having to take a portable printer with them. In an emergency, you can fax a document to yourself at your hotel. It won't be pretty, but it will be hard copy.

What to Use When You Need to Take a Printer with You

Some users are seriously impeded without a printer. If that is the case, consider the GCC WriteMove II. It weighs only 2.5 pounds and the output is excellent and costs only $.25 per page. Fewer users in this category really need PostScript, but for those who do, the best solution is the Mannesmann Tally MOBILEWriterPS. It is about a pound heavier than a 100-series PowerBook and has roughly the same form factor. This ingenious device uses a thermal transfer print engine that's rated at 6 pages per minute and includes a paper tray that can hold up to 80 pages. It needs very smooth surface paper, but yields respectable output. The cost per page is a modest $.10.

A Dock for Non-Duo PowerBooks

One of the several neat features of the Duo is its docking ability. But that doesn't mean 100-series PowerBook users are left out. BookEndz from Pilot Technology is a dock that accommodates almost any cable you're likely to plug into the back of a PowerBook. So instead of wrestling with several cables and connectors, you simply slide the PowerBook into BookEndz when you return to home base, and slide it out when it's time to hit the road again. In addition to making the entire process faster and more convenient, it has the added benefit of reducing wear and stress on the PowerBook connectors.

Do You Need a Car Alarm for Your PowerBook?

We don't have a lot of faith in commercial security devices for the PowerBook, perhaps because we live in an urban environment where car alarms deter only amateurs, and every bike thief knows that a Volvo jack will snap an expensive Kryptonite-brand lock in seconds. If you believe in security devices, you can use the Kensington MicroSaver, a 6-foot cable device that you can use to secure the PowerBook to some less portable object. There are even audio alarms that sound quite loudly whenever the armed PowerBook is moved. (SonicPro PowerBook Alarm from SonicPro International is a good one.) You, however, are the best PowerBook security device. Keep it in your sight, on your person, or locked in a hotel safe at all times when traveling.

Keeping Your Duo Dock Files to Yourself

The Duo dock includes a lock, which prevents anyone from removing your Duo while it's docked. You can also keep anyone from inserting their Duo into your dock in your absence if you lock it after you remove your Duo. This strategy prevents anyone from inserting a Duo into your dock and exploring the files on your dock's internal drive at will.

A Recommended Purchase Only for PowerBook 145B Owners

With the PowerBook 145B, Apple shipped its first PowerBook without a set of System installation disks. This cost-cutting policy helped make the 145B the least expensive PowerBook in the current lineup by saving Apple entire cents of manufacturing costs. (At press time there were rumors that future models of the PowerBook would also exclude System disks, a questionable policy Apple first introduced with the Performa Macs that it sells through mass-market retailers.) We applaud less expensive PowerBooks, but every Mac owner needs a complete set of System disks, so we recommend that you purchase a set when you buy your 145B. This saves you the hassle of having to make the purchase when the day inevitably arrives when you have to reinstall the System.

A Recommended First Step Only for PowerBook 145B Owners Who Don't Follow Tip 368

The importance of backing up your hard disk takes on an added urgency when you purchase a PowerBook 145B and don't follow the advice to purchase a set of System disks, as described in Tip 368. Since you don't own a set of System installation disks, you're courting disaster if you don't back up the hard drive, using either the HD Backup utility on the Disk Tools disk or a commercial backup utility such as DiskFit, Retrospect, or FastBack.

When to Sleep

There's a lot of confusion in the PowerBook community about system sleep, and Apple is responsible for a good portion of it. Apple's documentation says that you shouldn't hit the road with a sleeping PowerBook because pressing a key by accident will wake it up. The experience of many thousands of PowerBook users shows that the odds of pressing a key, either by accident or on purpose, when the PowerBook is closed are statistically insignificant. We've carried sleeping PowerBooks from place to place for well over a year with no ill effects.

When to Shut Down

TIP 371

There are only a few times when you absolutely must shut down your PowerBook: when you're connecting a SCSI cable (this includes SCSI docking), when you're connecting an external monitor, and when you're inserting a Duo into its Dock. Note that this includes connecting and removing. You should also shut down when you're not going to be using the PowerBook for longer than a day. This is particularly true if the AC adapter isn't connected. In this case, the battery drains, albeit at an almost imperceptible rate.

File-Synchronization Utilities

TIP 372

Synchronizing files between a desktop Mac and a PowerBook is an unpleasant subject that is only partially addressed by the commercial file-synchronization utilities available. They all work, to one degree or another, but they all suffer the same flaw: They can recognize when the same file has been modified on both machines, but they can't reconcile the two. It's up to you to decide whether you want to keep the one with the latest modification date. Our experience is that file-synching utilities are only useful if your work habits are such that you're confident that files will only be changed on one "side" of the process. Two general-purpose PowerBook utility programs, Symantec's Norton Essentials for the PowerBook and Connectix CPU 2.0, include file synching features. You might also be interested in one of the file-synching utilities on the market. These include MBS Technologies' FileRunner, Inline Design's Inline Sync, Leader Technologies' PowerMerge, and Qdea's Synchronize.

The Simplest Synchronization Tip of All Time

Keeping files synchronized between two Macs isn't particularly simple. The Finder doesn't provide any real tools for the task, and the file synching utilities we've seen still require you to intervene from time to time. Our favorite solution, which we first encountered in *The PowerBook Companion, 2nd Edition* (Addison-Wesley, 1993) by Richard Wolfson and Sharon Zardetto Aker, is a model of simplicity itself: After you copy a file from your desktop Mac to your PowerBook, delete the original on the desktop Mac. When it's time to work with that file on the desktop Mac, repeat the procedure, deleting the copy on your PowerBook after the copy. Since we adopted this strategy as our own, we haven't felt the need to use any special file-synchronization utility.

How to Share Files Between a Desktop Mac and a PowerBook

The most efficient way to share files between your desktop Mac and your PowerBook depends on whether or not your Mac supports SCSI Disk Mode. The PowerBook 100 and second-generation PowerBooks numbered 160 and above all have this feature, which lets you mount the PowerBook's hard drive on the desktop Mac. (To enable SCSI Disk Mode, shut down both machines. Attach the SCSI Disk Mode cable that shipped with the PowerBook to the PowerBook and the desktop Mac's SCSI chain. Next boot the PowerBook; then the desktop Mac.)

If your PowerBook does not support SCSI Disk Mode, the preferred way to share files between the two is to use System 7 File Sharing.

Getting Through Airport Security the Fast, Easy Way

Getting a PowerBook through airport security safely isn't nearly as complicated or dangerous as you might think. Although x-rays can't damage your computer, the magnetic field generated by the conveyer belt motor can. Metal detectors are also incompatible with PowerBooks. The solution is to ask the nice agent to visually inspect your PowerBook. He or she will certainly ask you to turn it on, so you can save time if your PowerBook is sleeping. If you find you've forgotten to put it in sleep mode, you can still save time by holding down the SHIFT key during the boot process. This trick allows startup without loading all those extensions you probably use, so the process is dramatically faster. After you've satisfied the security agent, put the PowerBook to sleep, so you can get back to work as quickly as possible when your plane reaches cruising altitude.

Where to Go for More Information

PowerBooks have arguably done more to increase the usefulness of the Mac as a productivity tool than any other single innovation. Just about any task you undertake on a Mac has a special consideration when you do it on a PowerBook. The single best source of information is *The PowerBook Companion, 2nd edition*, (Addison-Wesley, 1993) by Richard Wolfson and Sharon Zardetto Aker. It covers the bases of the entire PowerBook product line logically, concisely, and accurately and in a thoroughly readable fashion. If you're trying to decide which PowerBook model to buy, this is the place to begin your homework. If you already own a PowerBook, it will serve you well as your primary resource.

APPENDIX A

A

Glossary

In addition to defining a number of terms used throughout this book, this glossary includes many other standard Macintosh terms, particularly concerning elements of the Macintosh user interface. It also includes some tips and recommendations for software.

32-bit addressing   The ability of some Macs to handle memory (RAM) addresses 4 bytes long. This gives them the ability to deal with up to 4 gigabytes (4 billion K) of RAM. Macs without this ability are limited to 8 Mb of RAM (up to 13 with Virtual Memory). Not all Macs capable of 32-bit addressing can use 4Gb of RAM; other factors, such as the number of sockets for RAM chips, can limit the amount of RAM in the Mac.

On Macs capable of 32-bit addressing, this feature can be enabled or disabled using the Memory control panel.

32-bit clean   An application, control panel, extension, or other program or utility that can run when the Mac has 32-bit addressing enabled.

Accelerator   A device added to the Macintosh to make it run faster. These devices usually replace the computer's central processing unit with another of a faster clock rate, or a different type of processor. For example, an accelerator might replace a 68020 or 68030 processor with a 68040 processor.

We have had good experience with DayStar accelerators for Macintosh II models. For models that have a Processor Direct Slot, the DayStar accelerators are on cards that fit into those slots. For other Macintosh models, DayStar makes a device that replaces the original CPU with a connector for their accelerator card. We were impressed with DayStar's clear documentation, ease of installation, and compatibility. We are also impressed with DayStar's upgrade offers; at any time, you can upgrade to a newer accelerator for the difference in price between the older and newer accelerator.

Access privileges   The rights a network user has for a shared folder or network volume. These rights are assigned by the owner of a folder. They include the ability to see files in a folder, make changes to the folder (including saving files in it), and to see folders within the folder.

Active window   The active window in any application is the window that displays the set of parallel lines running across the window's title bar.

Adobe Type Manager (ATM)   This control panel allows PostScript fonts to be displayed on screen in virtually any size without jaggies. It also allows fonts of any size to be printed smoothly on virtually any printer, even if that printer does not have PostScript built in.

Alert box   A special class of dialog box containing a warning or error message. Alerts typically appear when an action will cause the loss of data that cannot be Undone. An example of an alert is shown here:

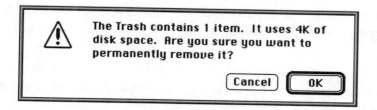

This alert appears when you empty the trash and have not disabled Trash Warnings.

Alias file   An alias is a small file that contains a "pointer" to the original of that file. When you open the icon of an alias, the Macintosh locates the original of that alias and opens it instead. Aliases allow you to make files appear to be in two places at once, and place files and folders so they are more conveniently located. Besides files and folders, you can make aliases of floppy disks (or other removable disks such as Syquest, optical, CD-ROM discs, and Bernoulli cartridges).

AOCE—Apple Open Collaboration Environment   A set of Apple system extensions, due in late 1993, that will allow Mac developers to add standard electronic mail features to their software.

Apple Desktop Bus (ADB)   The mechanism by which input devices such as keyboards, mice, trackballs, and graphics tablets are connected to the Macintosh. Like SCSI, devices can be daisy-chained to one another.

Apple events   Apple events are messages that can be sent from program to program, allowing one program to control another. Unless you are using a scripting system such as AppleScript or Frontier, or some capabilities of a macro utility such as QuicKeys or Tempo, Apple events require little or no user interaction.

Apple File Exchange (AFE)   An Apple utility that allows the Macintosh to read and write disks formatted by MS-DOS-based computers or Apple IIs, and which can also translate documents between various formats. AFE is a confusing program to use. A better solution is to use a utility such as PC Exchange to mount DOS disks to the desktop and a translation utility such as MacLink Plus/PC to translate the documents.

Apple Menu Items folder   One of System 7's special System Folder folders. Items placed in the Apple Menu Items folder display their names and icons on the Apple menu and are opened when you choose them from that menu. This folder is created automatically by the Finder; if you delete it from your disk or move it outside the System Folder, the Apple Menu Items folder automatically reappears.

AppleScript   AppleScript consists of several extensions that let you control the Macintosh and the applications running on it using an English language-like syntax. AppleScript is available now to developers, and will be available in a user package in the Fall of 1993.

AppleShare   AppleShare is Apple's software that allows a Macintosh to be a dedicated server for sharing files with a large number of Macintoshes. It differs from System 7 file sharing, in that it more or less takes over the Macintosh on which it is running and allows for many more users.

AppleShare volumes are accessed by using the Chooser. Other network server products can make themselves "look like" AppleShare servers, allowing users to use the same mechanisms for connecting with those servers. These include servers such as Novell's NetWare.

AppleTalk   The software protocols that allow Macs to communicate with other Macs (or other computers) using network cabling. This software, built into all Macs, is independent of the cabling architecture itself, though different cabling architectures might require additional software (which is distributed as an extension or control panel).

Application menu   The menu at the far right of the menu bar. It allows you to switch between applications and hide their windows. The menu name is always a small icon of the program in front, and a check mark appears next to the name of the current application on the menu, as shown here:

Holding down the OPTION key while switching between applications hides the current application's windows. The names and icons of applications whose windows are hidden are displayed in gray on the menu.

Hiro Yamamoto's ApplWindows is a terrific control panel that adds hierarchical menus to each application, allowing you to switch to specific windows within those applications.

Application program   A program used for a specific purpose, such as a graphics program, word processor, or a spreadsheet.

ASCII   American Standard Code for Information Interchange. The standard means of encoding which numbers refer to which characters (including letters, numbers, many typographical symbols, and so on) in the computer, and for exchange between computers and programs that cannot read one another's file format. ASCII is used for online communications, too.

ASCII is also commonly called "text only," and files saved in this format usually do not include information about styles—such as bold, italic, and underlined—as ASCII does not include a means of defining these styles. ASCII also does not include a *complete* character set as used on the Macintosh, so many symbols cannot be encoded in standard ASCII.

Background application   1) An application not currently the foreground (or frontmost) application. 2) An application specifically designed to run in the background.

Background printing   The ability of the Macintosh to print documents while allowing you to do work in another active application. You enable Background Printing when you choose a printer using the Chooser.

Backing store   The file used to store data held by a virtual memory utility. The backing store is used to simulate memory above and beyond the actual RAM in the computer. System 7's Memory control panel creates an invisible file called "VM Storage" as its backing store.

Backing up   The act of making a copy of valuable data to have in case disaster strikes. Backing up includes manually making copies of important files on floppy disks or network volumes, and using dedicated backup applications to back up entire hard disks to floppy disks, cartridge drives, or tape drives.

Balloon help   Apple's help mechanism for System 7. When you choose the Show Balloons item on the Help menu, small balloons appear next to many screen items (such as menu items, icons, and controls), offering definitions of the purposes of those items. The presence of the balloons does not affect the operation of programs, other than slowing them down a little.

Balloon help is most useful for cases when you do not use a program often or see devices in its windows that you do not understand.

Developers can also add an item to the Help menu to provide a means of getting at more detailed help. For example, the Finder provides more detailed help about its shortcuts on the Help menu.

Baud   Often used (incorrectly) as a term indicating the speed of a modem. Instead, use "bits per second," and see that definition.

BBS—Bulletin Board System   A BBS is a computer (or computers) set up to allow others to connect to it over the telephone with a modem. The system runs special software that presents those who call with an interface that allows them to exchange messages and files. There are approximately 40,000 BBSs in the United States.

Bernoulli cartridge drive   A removable cartridge drive system from Iomega Corp. Unlike hard disk drives, the Bernoulli cartridge uses a flexible media for the drive platter. Hard disk level performance is achieved by controlling the position of the media surface relative to the drive's read/write mechanism using the Bernoulli principle of physics (an increase in the speed of a fluid produces a decrease in pressure and a decrease in the speed produces an increase in pressure, if you're curious). Bernoulli cartridges are less fragile than Syquest cartridges, which use a fixed platter.

Bitmap font   A font whose design exists as a pattern of bits (also called pixels), in a specific size. While the font can be scaled to appear in different sizes, that scaling will not be effective unless there is also a TrueType of PostScript version of the font available.

Bitmap graphics   Graphics, of the type produced by "paint" programs, or acquired by scanners, which are composed entirely of dots on the screen. These dots may be white, black, or any of millions of other colors. (*See* Object graphics.)

Boot volume   *See* Startup volume.

BPS (bits per second)   The number of bits that a modem can transmit in one second. A bit is a single on or off code. Eight bits compose a single byte, which is a single ASCII letter or number. Modern modems are available that communicate at 2400, 9600, and 14,400 bits per second.

Bridge   A device that connects two or more separate networks to one another. The subnetworks that are connected are called zones.

Bulletin Board   *See* BBS.

Cache   1) An area of memory used to hold items frequently requested from disk. You can control the size of the Mac's built-in cache using the Memory control panel. 2) Special memory used to contain data and instructions frequently used by the processor. Special cache cards, containing this memory, are available for most Macs with Processor Direct Slots (PDS).

Carpal Tunnel Syndrome   A serious repetitive stress injury of the wrist. The nine tendons that control the wrist and fingers slide back and forth in a tunnel called the Carpal Tunnel. These tendons become irritated from many activities, included long, interrupted sessions with a keyboard and mouse.

Cartridge drive   A drive encased in a cartridge, and providing hard disk-like storage capabilities and speed (unlike floppy disks which do not have high capacity or speed). The cartridges are removable, giving you greater storage capacity than hard disks. Cartridge drives include SyQuest drives, Bernoulli cartridges, and optical drives.

CD-ROM   Compact Disc-Read Only Memory. CD-ROM is an increasingly popular medium for large amounts of data (several hundred megabytes). Photos, QuickTime movies, dictionaries, entire encyclopedias and other large works are often available in CD-ROM format. A computer CD-ROM drive is read only, that is, you cannot write to the disk.

cdev   An old term for control panel device.

Character   A letter of the alphabet, digit, or other symbol, that can be displayed on the screen or stored by the computer. A character is equal to 1 byte of RAM or disk storage.

Check box   An item in the Macintosh user interface that allows you to enable or disable an option. The option is enabled when the box is filled with an X and disabled otherwise, as shown here:

LaserWriter 8.0 Options	8.0	OK
Visual Effects:		Cancel
☐ Flip Horizontal		
☐ Flip Vertical		Help
☐ Invert Image		
Printer Options:		
☒ Substitute Fonts		
☒ Smooth Text		
☒ Smooth Graphics		
☐ Precision Bitmap Alignment (4% reduction)		
☐ Larger Print Area (Fewer Downloadable Fonts)		
☐ Unlimited Downloadable Fonts in a Document		

Clicking on an empty check box places the X in it; clicking on it again removes the X.

Note that the check boxes are independent of one another (unlike radio buttons). In well-implemented Mac programs, you are not required to click directly in the box; you can click anywhere on the box's label.

Chooser   Located in the Apple Menu Items folder (and thus on the Apple menu), the Chooser allows you to select which network devices you wish to use. These include such things as AppleShare servers, networked laser printers, and other devices such as shared modems. In addition to networked laser printers, you use it to choose between printers attached directly to your Macintosh.

Clipboard   The transparent-to-you location in memory (and sometimes on disk) in which the Mac holds data you have cut or copied. Remember that the Clipboard will only hold *one item at a time*. That is, when you cut or copy something, the Clipboard's previous contents are replaced by the new contents.

Clipboard file   Maintained in the System Folder, this file holds the contents of the Clipboard when it becomes too large to be held in RAM.

COMMAND key   A modifier key labeled with the ⌘ symbol and sometimes also with an open (hollow) Apple.

Comments   When you select a file and use the Get Info command, the window that results includes an area in which you can type comments about that file. Do *not* use these comments. They could be useful, but they are erased when you rebuild the desktop.

Commercial software   Software available for a license fee through for-profit distribution channels. Compare to shareware, freeware, and public-domain software.

Compatibility Checker   A HyperCard application shipped with System 7 that tests the applications, control panels, and extensions on your hard disk against its own records to make sure they are compatible with the latest version of the system. The compatibility checker is of limited use, as its information is generally somewhat out of date.

Component   A component is a special type of driver or utility that is added to the Extensions folder, and is used by another utility (such as QuickTime or AppleScript). QuickTime uses various components to support different compression mechanisms or devices for acquiring video. AppleScript uses components to add new features to the language, or support alternative scripting languages.

Compressor—QuickTime   A program that compresses (makes smaller) data of a particular type, such as photos, sound, or moving images. Many compressors are built into QuickTime, and others can be added by putting them into the Extensions folder.

CONTROL key   One of the four modifier keys. The others are OPTION, ⌘, and SHIFT.

Control panel   Like an extension, a control panel often contains special programming that is loaded into the Mac's memory when it starts up, and adds features to the Macintosh or modifies its behavior. However, control panels generally have options that you can set by double-clicking on them. They are located in the Control Panels folder inside the System Folder.

Data fork   The portion of a file in the Mac's two-fork file system that generally contains the data portion of a document (though some programmers store data in the resource fork, against their better judgment). Most programs will not contain data forks, while most documents will be almost entirely data forks.

Database   A type of program used to store regular items of information. There are, in general, two types of these programs, although the second is not generally marketed as a database.

A *general* database, such as FileMaker Pro, Panorama, 4th Dimension, and others, allows you (or a database programmer) to define the types of data the program works with. For example, a name and address book would include *fields* (specific items of information) for such things as first name, last name, street address, city, and so on.

A *specialized* database is set up to let you record specific types of information. This type of database includes personal information managers (storing names and addresses, appointment logs, and so on) and financial programs. These specialized types of databases are not marketed as databases.

Default   The standard behavior of a program or utility, or a standard setting. For example, most word processors have default fonts, margins, and font styles for new documents. Often these defaults can be changed using a Preferences command.

Desk accessory   Before System 7, a desk accessory was a special kind of small program, which was stored inside the System file itself, whose name appeared on the Apple menu. A special utility called Font/DA Mover was required to install a desk accessory. In System 7, desk accessories as a specific type of program, have disappeared; older desk accessories appear to System 7 users as programs, and anything can be made to appear in the Apple menu by placing it (or an alias of it) in the Apple Menu Items folder.

The icons of old style desk accessories are small suitcases. You can convert an old-style desk accessory to an application by double-clicking on the suitcase to open it (like a folder), and dragging the item that appears in the suitcase window out of the suitcase folder. These converted desk accessories do not usually have their own icons, and cannot generally accept files dropped on top of them.

Desktop   The "top level" of the Macintosh environment, which you see in the Finder, or in Open or Save dialog boxes. The Desktop includes all mounted volumes and the trash can.

Desktop file   In System 6, the Macintosh maintained an invisible file called "desktop" that was used to store many items about files, such as its position within a window and its Finder comments. In System 7, this single file is replaced by two files called Desktop DF and Desktop DB, which are more efficient.

Developer   The individual or company that designs and usually markets a software product.

Dialog box   A box containing a message, often asking for more information or requiring feedback from you before proceeding. Examples include the Page Setup and Print dialog boxes, as well as those summoned by the Open or Save As commands.

There are two broad categories of dialog boxes. Modal dialog boxes do not allow you to do other things while the box is available; these dialog boxes usually do not have standard title bars on their windows, and may not be moved. Nonmodal dialog boxes (such as those used for Find commands in many word processors) allow you to click outside them to bring other windows to the fore.

Disk allocation   1) The amount of room a file takes up on disk. 2) The size of blocks allocated by the file system. As discussed in Tip 257, the Mac file system writes data to the disk in blocks, and allocates a complete block, whether or not the file uses all of that block. (*See also* Desktop files.)

Disk cache   *See* cache.

Dithering   A process of removing colors from an image while maintaining the appearance of a large number of colors. Pixels of different colors are placed next to one another so that they appear to blend together and look like different colors.

Document   In general, a document is any file on a Macintosh disk that is not an application program. More specifically, a document is a file containing information you have created and saved in a file.

DOS   Disk Operating System. In general, this refers to any computer operating system (Apple II computers used a version called "DOS 3.3"), but more specifically it refers to Microsoft's DOS for

Intel-based, IBM-compatible personal computers. This operating system is called MS-DOS or, on IBM-brand PCs, PC-DOS.

Double-clicking   The act of clicking the mouse button twice in rapid succession. In the Finder, this is a shortcut for using the Open command on a file, application or folder. In other applications, double-clicking on text is a shortcut for selecting an entire word.

Downloading   The act of transferring a file from a remote computer to a local computer. The term usually refers to cases where the two computers are connected by modem, but can also refer to network connections.

Draw graphics   Also called object graphics. Graphics produced by programs in which everything is stored as a mathematical representation of the object you draw. For example, when using a drawing program, a rectangle is stored using numbers representing the top-left and bottom-right corners of the rectangle; you can resize this rectangle later. Contrast to paint graphics, in which images are composed solely of discrete pixels.

Draw program   A program that creates draw-type graphics. While these programs generally do not support all the effects that can be gained through a painting program, they are useful for such things as creating flyers, ad material, and sometimes newsletters or other text documents that contain multiple columns, graphics, and/or text boxes.

Drivers   Programs—usually system extensions—that allow the Macintosh to communicate with devices such as printers, modems, removable drives (such as CD-ROM drives or SyQuest cartridges), scanners, and the like.

Easy Access   An optional Finder feature provided by Apple that makes operating the Macintosh easier for many with disabilities, and providing some handy features for all users.

Edition   An edition file is the product of the act of publishing a selection of a document when using a program that supports publish and subscribe. The edition can then be accessed by applications that support subscribing.

Electronic mail (e-mail)   Messages sent to others, using only computers. The target of the message may be another user on the same network, in which case network e-mail programs, such as CE Software's QuickMail, are used. The other user might have an address on an online service, in which case the address used by that person must be known.

Enabler   A special extension residing in the System Folder. Enablers are produced to allow the System to run on certain Macintoshes, or to add features to older Macs. Enablers permit Apple to introduce new Mac models without having to release simultaneously a new version of the System.

EPS   Encapsulated PostScript. A file format for storing graphics, in which the graphics are rendered in the PostScript programming language. The file can also include a PICT version of the graphic, to allow Macintosh programs to display the graphic on screen. EPS files are also supported by many PC programs, so the file format is a good one for translating graphics. However, EPS files are much larger than strictly binary versions of the files.

When using the LaserWriter 8.0 (from Apple) or PSWriter printer drivers, you can create an EPS file from virtually any program.

Ethernet   A high-speed network architecture. Many Macintoshes and Apple laser printers have built-in connectors for Ethernet hardware, and it can be added to others. The Ethernet architecture is faster and more flexible than Apple's LocalTalk architecture, but also more expensive. The software allowing Macs to use Ethernet services is called EtherTalk.

Extension   Extensions (formerly called INITs) are programs that load into the Macintosh's memory when it starts, and add capabilities to the virgin system software. Extensions can include drivers that allow the Macintosh to communicate with devices such as scanners, CD-ROM drives, and printers. They also add features to the system, such as the QuickTime and AppleScript extensions.

Extensions folder   One of System 7's special folders inside the System folder. This folder contains Extensions that load when the Mac starts up (such as disk drivers and utilities such as QuickTime), as well as printer drivers.

Fast Save format   An optional format for saving files with Microsoft Word. Avoid this format option; choose Normal format instead. Fast Save Word files usually cannot be read by other word processors and result in larger files than Word's Normal format.

FDHD (super floppy)   The 1.4Mb floppy disk drive Apple has included with most new Macintoshes for some time. The SuperDrive is capable of reading and writing older 800K Macintosh disks and, when the Mac is running the necessary software, MS-DOS disks.

Field   The components of a database record. For example, a single record of a name and address database might contain individual fields for the name, address and phone number.

File sharing   Built into System 7, File Sharing is the ability of any Macintosh to share volumes and folder folders with other Macintoshes connected to it on a network.

File   A collection of data stored in one unit on a Mac disk. In general, there are two kinds of files: programs (including extensions, control panel., and applications) and documents.

File server   Any Mac, or other computer, that has made portions of its hard disk or disks available to other users on a network.

Finder   The application that is launched automatically whenever your Macintosh is started and presents you with your Desktop.

Finder views   The set of items available on the Finder's View menu, which determines how files are displayed and sorted in a folder.

FKey   A small program that is part of your System file. FKeys are activated by pressing certain keystroke combinations. The standard FKey built into every System file is the ⌘-SHIFT-3 key combination, which saves a TeachText PICT file of the current screen (of the current window if the CAPS LOCK key is also down).

Floating-point unit (FPU)   A secondary processor in some Macintoshes, designed to work with numeric operations, particularly those which use floating-point numbers (not integers). If you do not make heavy use of numbers, or do not use software that requires it, do not worry if your Mac does not have an FPU in it.

Font   In Macintosh usage, a font is a set of letters, numbers, punctuation marks, and other symbols with a name defining them and a consistent appearance. In standard typesetting parlance, this is actually a *typeface*, and each variation on the typeface is a font. For example, in traditional typesetting parlance, Geneva 10 point is one face, while Geneva 9 point is another, and Geneva 10 point italic is a third. Remembering the difference between the two uses of the term is important.

Foreground application   The *foreground* application is the one whose windows are not hidden by the windows of other applications. Its name appears with a check mark on the Application menu.

Fragmentation, disk   As files are deleted from a hard disk, empty spaces are left on the disk. When new files are written to that disk, they take up empty spaces. A file might not fit exactly into a specific empty space, so separate portions of it—fragments—are written to separate empty blocks. Over time, many files can become fragmented, leading to slower disk access as the disk's read/write head must move to many locations to read a single file. A disk can be defragmented by backing it up, formatting, and restoring it, or by running a commercial defragmenting utility (such as those available in Symantec's Norton Utilities or Central Point's MacTools).

Fragmentation, memory   When you quit from an application, the area of memory occupied by that application is freed. But applications using memory adjacent to the area used by the other program do not move to take up the space it left, so memory becomes fragmented. The only way to defragment memory is to quit from all running applications and start them again.

Freeware   Software for which the author still maintains copyright, but no license fee is required. Not to be confused with shareware.

Function key   Any of the keys labeled F1 through F15 (or higher) on extended keyboards. These keys may be used by software developers to give access to application functions without using menus.

GIF format   Graphics Interchange Format. This format was developed by CompuServe as a standard format for graphics that could be read by any system. GIF files are limited to 8-bit color (256 colors), and can be read by a wide variety of Macintosh programs.

Gigabyte (Gb)   1 billion bytes, 1000Mb.

Handshaking   Handshaking is the process by which two devices (notably a Macintosh and a modem, or two modems) establish communications. When a modem dials and is answered by another modem, a series of tones are sent between the two to establish the speed at which they are communicating. You can hear these tones unless you have turned you modem's sound off.

Heap   *See* System heap.

Highlight   To select something. Selected icons in the Finder, selected text in word processors, and selected items in other applications are often displayed in a different color than non-selected items. You can change the color used for highlighting with the Color control panel.

HyperCard   An application developed by Bill Atkinson, released in August of 1987, and included, in one form or another, with every Macintosh shipped since.

HyperCard is a kind of database application, in which data appears as a stack of cards. The data can be regular (as in a standard database, where each card stores the same kind of data) or very flexible (in which case each card contains its own kind of data). Graphics can also be stored on the card.

What made HyperCard special was its *scripting language*, which allowed, for basically the first time, nonprogrammers to create Macintosh documents that in many ways behaved as applications in their own right.

Though originally an Apple project, HyperCard was turned over to Claris in 1990 to be marketed and supported separately. Claris was unsuccessful in selling the product, and since it wasn't making any money with it, it didn't put a lot back into research and development to create new versions of it. In early 1993, Apple took HyperCard back from Claris, and is revising it. A new version is due in late 1993, which will add color and AppleScript support.

HyperCard is now bundled with new Macs in a "player" version which cannot create new documents nor edit old stacks (it can only "play" or view existing stacks). The full Claris version is available in retail. The current version at press time is 2.1.

Icon   A graphical representation of a disk, file, or folder on the Macintosh desktop or in a window.

Info window   The window displayed by the Finder when you select an item and use the Get Info command. This window tells you the name of the file, its creation and modification dates, and its version number. It also displays an area into which you can write comments. (*See* Tip 14.)

If the file shown is an application, this window also lets you adjust the amount of memory (RAM) the program will request when it starts.

If the file is an alias, the window includes a button which locates the original of the alias file, and opens the window containing that file.

INIT   An old term for an Extension.

Installer   The utility program that installs software on your hard disk.

Integrated software   Software performing a variety of functions, containing, in effect, small versions of standard Macintosh application categories. A typical integrated program includes a word processor, a spreadsheet, a database, a drawing and/or painting program, and a communications program.

Integrated software is a good choice in several cases. First, when you first get a computer, an integrated program is a good way to get started in several application categories without spending a lot of money. As your needs grow, you can purchase, for example, a more powerful word processor, while still using the spreadsheet and database portion of the integrated program. You might only grow out of one part of the program.

Second, an integrated program is a good choice when you are using a portable computer (whether you have a desktop computer or not). An integrated program will require less disk space than a set of dedicated programs, and be more suited to life away from the office. If you *do* also have a desktop machine, and are using different files on it, make sure it and the integrated program can read each others' files. The major products in this category are ClarisWorks (recommended) and Microsoft Works (not recommended).

Invisible file   A file that is not visible in a Finder window. Files are usually made invisible so that users do not inadvertently delete them. Common invisible files are the VM Storage file used by Virtual Memory, and the Desktop DB and Desktop DF files used to hold desktop information. Several programs, such as Apple's ResEdit, let you make invisible files visible and vice versa.

jpg format   Also called jpeg. A compression format used for graphics, mostly for scanned pictures. JPEG is mostly designed for 24-bit graphics, and achieves compression ratios of up to 100 to 1, depending on a "quality" parameter. The format is "lossy," meaning that data is lost when the image is compressed. How much data is lost is controlled by the quality parameter.

Keyboard equivalent   A combination of keystrokes that performs the same action as choosing a command from a menu. Keyboard equivalents most commonly use the ⌘ key in conjunction with another key, but can also use combinations involving the OPTION, CONTROL, and SHIFT keys.

Kilobyte 1024 bytes.

List view Any of the views available on the View in the Finder that shows the names of files in a list. These items include views by name, date, kind, and label.

LocalTalk A low-cost, low-speed networking architecture used for connecting Macintoshes to other Macintoshes (and PCs equipped with the necessary hardware) and printers. LocalTalk connections are built into all Macintoshes, and only require the addition of a small box to the Macintosh and the correct cabling. LocalTalk cabling is available from Apple, and a number of other vendors also make LocalTalk connectors available; notable among them are those which use standard telephone wires. These connectors are called "phone connectors" and are available from Farallon, Novatech, and others.

MacBinary format A format in which the two forks of many Macintosh files (data fork and resource fork), as well as Finder information such as icons, label, and modification date, are encoded in a single file for use by systems (such as online services) which do not support dual-fork systems.

Macintosh Easy Open An Apple extension and control panel combination that works with third-party utilities (such as DataViz' MacLink Plus/PC) to provide nearly transparent translation of documents between a variety of formats.

Macro A special kind of keyboard equivalent or shortcut that performs a wide variety of actions, including typing text, giving commands, and the like, with a single key combination. Many application programs support macros of their own, and utilities such as CE Software's QuicKeys and Affinity MicroSystems' Tempo, provide generalized macro capabilities to all programs.

Megabyte 1,000 kilobytes—1,024,000 bytes.

Megahertz A measure of the speed of a chip.

Memory Memory is the RAM storage built into the Macintosh. The system itself, application programs, and documents are loaded into RAM while in use. RAM is different from disk storage.

Menu A list of related commands that is accessed with the mouse, and sometimes also with the keyboard. Menu names usually appear across the top of the screen, and are listed from left to right.

Menu bar   The 20-pixel high white bar that runs across the Macintosh's main monitor (on systems with several monitors, the menu bar appears only on one of them). The menubar contains pull-down menus, which you use to give commands to applications.

Mode32   A control panel—produced by Connectix and distributed free by Apple—that gives older Macintosh models (such as the Mac II, IIx, IIcx, SE/30 and others) the ability to work in 32-bit mode, allowing them access to more memory.

Modem   A device that connects the computer to standard telephone lines, and allows it to communicate with other computers. Modems modulate digital data, which computers know how to understand, to a series of tones which can be broadcast over telephone lines, and also demodulate those tones to digital information.

Modems are usually differentiated by their speeds, which are measured in bits per second. Common speeds are 2400, 9600, and 14,400 (14.4K) bits per second.

Modifier key   A key that, when held down, affects the behavior of another key pressed while the modifier is held down. For example, the SHIFT key is a modifier key that changes the a to an A. The other standard modifier keys on the Macintosh keyboard are the ⌘ key (typically used for keyboard equivalents), OPTION key (generally for producing international or typographical characters, but also used for commands or for modifying the effects of mouse actions), and the CONTROL key.

Modal dialog   *See* Dialog box.

Monospaced font   A font in which the characters have the same width. Courier and Monaco are two monospaced fonts that are standard Mac issue. Compare with Proportional font.

Mount   The act of making a volume appear on the Macintosh desktop. When you start the Macintosh, its startup disk is mounted automatically, as are any connected SCSI hard disks that are turned on. Floppy disks are mounted automatically when they are inserted, and you use the Chooser to mount network disks.

Network   A connection between computers, printers, and other devices. Networked computers can share the use of printers and storage (using a network server or System 7 File Sharing), and when running special software, users can send electronic mail messages to one another.

Network zone   A logical grouping of computers, file servers, and other items on a network.

NuBus   An architecture present in most Macintosh II-class machines that allows addition of hardware to the Macintosh by plugging in special boards.

Numeric keypad   The portion of the keyboard that includes a standard ten-key layout for entering numbers and mathematical symbols (+,−,=, and so on). On some keyboards, such as the Apple Ergonomic Keyboard, the numeric keypad can be a separate device.

Object graphics   *See* Draw graphics.

OCR   Optical Character Recognition. Software that, with the help of a scanner, can import text from a printed document. You can them manipulate the imported text with any word processor.

OPTION key   A modifier key. The other modifier keys are ⌘ (COMMAND), CONTROL, and SHIFT.

OPTION-drag   The act of holding down the OPTION key while dragging with the mouse. Use OPTION-drag to make a copy of a selected file without moving the original.

Outline view   When Finder windows are set to be viewed in a list form (when the View menu is set to any item other than Icon or Small Icon).

Paged Memory Unit   *See* PMMU.

Paint program   A graphics program that generates bitmapped graphics as opposed to object-oriented graphics.

Parameter RAM   RAM in the Macintosh that is maintained by its battery and used to hold several settings (controlled by control panels) when the Macintosh is turned off.

Partition   A portion of the hard disk that has been separated from other portions of the hard disk. Each partition appears on the desktop as a separate volume.

PC   Though the term "personal computer" should be generic, in fact it refers specifically to IBM's Personal Computer, and those compatible with it (that is, a personal computer based on the Intel processor set and running Microsoft's DOS and/or Windows).

PhoneNet   A trademarked term of Farallon Computing, referring to their set of products which allow Macintoshes to be connected on a network with standard telephone wiring. Often incorrectly used generically to refer to any such product.

PICT format   The standard Macintosh graphics format, supported by virtually every Mac program capable of working with graphics. PICT files can contain bitmap, as well as draw-type or object graphics.

PIM   Personal Information Manager. A kind of program designed to facilitate maintenance of one or more of the following kinds of data: appointment books, address books, to-do lists, and schedules of all types.

Pixel   The smallest dot that can be seen on the screen or on the printer. Images are composed of patterns of pixels. Depending on the capabilities and settings of the monitor or printer, that dot can be white or black, or one of any number of colors.

PMMU—Paged Memory Unit   A processor required by older Macs (those with 68020 processors) that is used to facilitate memory management. Macs with 68000 processors *cannot* take advantage of the services of a PMMU, and Macs with 68030 and 68040 processors do not need one, as memory management is built into those chips.

Pointer   The pointer is the visual indicator on the screen that moves when you move the mouse. Depending on what you're doing on your Mac at the time, the pointer can be the arrow, the I-beam, the wristwatch, or spinning beach ball.

Pop-up menu   Menus that are displayed when you click their title. Pop-up menus usually appear in dialog boxes.

Posterizing   A graphics effect available in many graphics applications. It distorts an image in the style made popular during the hippie era.

PostScript   The device-independent page description language created by Adobe Systems, Inc., and built into many laser printers. QuickDraw is used instead on non-PostScript printers and the Mac screen.

PRAM   *See* Parameter RAM.

PrintMonitor   An application located in the Extensions folder that automatically sends documents to the printer when Background Printing is enabled. PrintMonitor starts automatically when spooled files appear in the PrintMonitor Documents folder in the System folder.

Processor direct slot   A special expansion slot, present on many Macintosh models that allows for more flexible and higher performance expansion than does NuBus. Unlike NuBus slots, the PDS is connected electronically directly to the processor.

Program linking   The ability of one program to send instructions (Apple events) to other programs running on separate Macintoshes connected by a network. Program Linking is enabled in general using the Sharing Setup control panel and granted or denied for individual users with the Users and Groups control panel.

Program   A set of instructions, not generally in human-readable format, that tells a computer what to do. There are many kinds of programs available on the Macintosh, such as application programs, extensions, control panels, and the like.

Programmer's switch   Actually two switches, located either on the right, left or rear of the Mac, depending on which model you have. The reset switch is used to restart the Mac if it is frozen (hung). The interrupt button is mainly used by programmers.

Proportional font   Any font in which the individual characters have different widths. An m is wider than an i, for example. Most fonts used on the Mac are proportionally spaced. Courier and Monaco are two notable exceptions. Compare to Monospaced font.

Public-domain software   Software for which the author has given up all rights. Compare to shareware, freeware, and commercial software.

Publisher   A portion of a document that has been made available to other documents through System 7's Publish and Subscribe technology. When a portion of a document has been published, an Edition file is created in a location of the user's choosing. Other documents can incorporate that edition, becoming Subscribers. When changes are made to the publisher, they are automatically, and very quickly, made part of all subscribers.

Pull-down menu   The standard Mac menu structure. These menus usually appear at the top of the screen. (*See* Menu.)

QuickDraw   The set of programs built into the Macintosh (in ROM and the System file) that are responsible for displaying everything that appears on the screen. Color QuickDraw is a set of extensions, present in Macintosh System Software since 1989, that are responsible for color management. QuickDraw GX is a forthcoming rewrite of QuickDraw that will overhaul the Mac's graphic architecture.

QuickDraw printer   Printers that rely on the Mac's QuickDraw to create the page image. Compare to PostScript.

QuickTime   A system extension which adds a wide variety of services to the Macintosh, including the ability to play and record video movies.

QuickTime compressor   Compressors are programs used by QuickTime to make images stored in it smaller. A number of compressors are built into QuickTime, and others can be added as extensions.

Radio button   A group of buttons in a dialog box. Only one button can be activated at a time. Compare to check boxes.

RAM   *See* Memory.

RAM disk   A portion of memory set aside and made to appear to be a disk volume. RAM disks offer great speed of access, but at the price of less reliability (their contents are cleared when the Mac shuts down).

Read Me file   A file distributed by software developers. It usually contains information about last-minute changes to the software that were made too late to include in the printed documentation. Most Read Me files are in the TeachText format.

Removable drive   *See* Cartridge drive.

ResEdit   A tool for editing resources contained in the resource forks of Macintosh files. Available through many online sources and user groups, and with most programming environments.

Resource   A numbered, often named, item contained in the Resource Fork of a Macintosh file (typically an application program or system software). Such items as icons, different pointer designs, text displayed in dialog boxes, dialog boxes themselves, and more, are usually defined as resources in a program. Resources can be edited with programs such as ResEdit.

Resource fork   That portion of a Macintosh file containing resources.

Restart   The command on the Finder's Special menu that causes your Macintosh to flush everything from memory and start over again. When a serious system error occurs, a button labeled Restart might also appear in a dialog box.

ROM   Read-Only Memory. Special chips inside the Macintosh containing programming that specifies its standard behavior. Macintoshes contain from 64K to 256K of ROM, and this ROM contains a lot of the programming that displays items on the screen.

Root level   A disk's top level.

Saving   The act of transferring data from the computer's RAM to disk. (Do it often.)

Scrapbook   A desk accessory, available to all programs as part of the standard set of system software, that can hold multiple items—text, pictures, sounds, movies. The Scrapbook is a good place to store items you use often—letterheads, signatures, logos, and the like.

Screen dump An image of the screen, saved in a file on disk. You can capture the Mac's screen by pressing ⌘-SHIFT-3, which is an FKey built into every Mac. This FKey *cannot* capture pulled down menus and cannot always capture the screen when dialog boxes are visible.

Captured screens are saved in files called Picture, with a number appended and saved at the root level of your startup disk. (In System 6, they were called Screen, with a number appended.) They are PICT files, and are opened by TeachText when you double-click them. You can also import them into any program that supports PICT files.

A number of utilities, such as MainStay's Capture and Nobu Toge's FlashIt, provide additional capabilities to screen capturing, such as the ability to capture pulled-down menus, name files, save them in different formats, and assign different creators to them.

Scrolling Scrolling is the act of changing which part of a document is visible within a window. It is accomplished through manipulating the scroll bar that appears at the right edge and/or bottom of a window.

At the top and bottom of the scroll bar (left and right of a horizontal scroll bar) are arrows. By clicking on these arrows, the document scrolls in small increments through the document—for example, in a word processor these usually scroll the document by a single line. Clicking on the gray area above or below the elevator box within the scroll bar scrolls by greater increments. Again, to use a word processor as an example, this will scroll by one screenful at a time. You can make bigger jumps by positioning the elevator box directly: drag it to a new location to position it. Its position within the gray area shows how much of the document lies above and below the current view of the window.

Script A set of instructions, created in a human-readable format, that instructs a program or programs to perform a set of actions. AppleScript and UserLand Frontier are two examples of scripting systems that can control a wide variety of applications. Scripts differ from macros in that macros are usually simple recordings of various actions, while scripts are written in a readable syntax, and can contain such things as variables, tests for certain conditions, and the like. (*See also* Macro.)

SCSI Small Computer Systems Interface. A standard mechanism for attaching other devices (such as hard disks, cartridge drives, CD-ROMs, and scanners) to the Macintosh. SCSI allows up to seven devices to be connected this way, in a "daisy chain." Each device has an ID or number between 0 and 6 (7 is reserved for the Macintosh itself); make sure that no two SCSI devices have the same ID.

Select   To make an object active, such as an icon in the Finder. An item is selected by clicking on it, or by dragging the mouse across items you want selected. Later commands—such as Cut or Copy, or various format commands—affect the selected object or objects.

Shared disk   A disk that is visible on the network and can be used by several users. Shared disks might be located on dedicated network servers (such as AppleShare servers) or might be made available by other users.

Shareware   Software that can be distributed freely, but for which the author asks payment if you use it.

SHIFT-clicking   The act of holding down the SHIFT key while clicking. SHIFT-clicking *extends* any selection to include the objects on which you click. In the Finder, you can click on a file, then SHIFT-click on any other file to select that file as well. In word processors, you can place the insertion point at one location (or select some text), and then SHIFT-click to select text between the original selection and the point at which you SHIFT-clicked.

Shut Down   The command on the Finder Special menu that powers down the computer. On some Mac models, the Shut Down command will only prepare the system be turned off, which you must do manually with the machine's on/off switch.

SIMMs   Single Inline Memory Modules. This is the standard form factor in which RAM is available for the Macintosh. These are called "strips" as each one will contain eight chips (a few Mac models can take advantage of strips that include nine chips).

Size box   The box at the bottom-right corner of Macintosh windows which is used to resize the window on the screen.

Splash screen   A dialog box or window that appears 1) when a program is first starting or 2) when you choose the "About" command on the Apple menu.

Spreadsheet   An application whose documents are organized into rows and columns. Numbers, dates, or text can be placed into any cell (the intersection of a row and column), along with formulas.

Stack   A HyperCard document.

Startup disk   The disk from which the Macintosh was started. It contains the currently active System Folder (that is, the System Folder containing the Finder that is currently running). If you have several hard disks, each with its own System Folder, you can choose to make any disk the Startup Disk by using the Startup Disk control panel and restarting the Macintosh.

Stationery   A file that is treated as a "template" by the Macintosh. Many programs allow you to save files as stationery pads. When you open such a file, it opens in an "Untitled" window, but that window contains all the information saved into that file. If the application does not directly support stationery pads, you can check the Stationery box in the file's Get Info window to change a document to stationery.

Subscriber   A document or portion of a document that includes an edition containing data published from another document.

Suitcase   With System 7.1, a file containing a font, including various versions of that font (such as TrueType and bitmap versions, along with different sizes and styles). Before System 7, fonts and desk accessories both were stored as suitcases.

Surge protector   A device into which you plug your Mac. It in turn is plugged into the wall. It protects your Mac from surges in the electricity supply you receive from your electricity company.

Syquest cartridge drive   One type of hard drive with removable cartridges.

Sysop   System Operator. One who maintains and manages a BBS system.

System file   The file inside the System Folder that contains the basic programming the Macintosh needs to start and operate. Besides this programming, the System file contains standard icons for alert boxes, sounds, FKeys, keyboard definitions, and more.

System Folder   A folder containing, at a minimum, a System file and other utilities needed by the System. Typically, these other utilities include the Finder, Extensions, Control Panels, and Fonts folders.

System heap   That portion of the Macintosh's RAM used by the System to provide basic services. It appears in the About This Macintosh display as the bar labeled "System Software," though this bar also includes memory used by the Finder.

System software   A general term for all the software which Apple includes with its Macintoshes and system software packages. It includes the System file itself, the Finder, and various control panels, desk accessories, extensions, printer drivers, and enablers.

Tab-delimited file   A file for holding structured data in ASCII format. The file consists of lines, separated by Return characters. Within each line, items are separated from one another by tab characters. When you export a database to this format, each line contains a record, and each item within that line is a field. When a spreadsheet file is exported to this format, each line is a row across the screen, and each item within the row is a cell on that row.

TeachText   An anemic application distributed with System Software by Apple. It provides a literal "lowest common denominator" file format for reading text and graphics. Most Read Me files describing last-minute changes made to software after the documentation was printed are provided in TeachText format.

Text editor   A program used for editing text. Differs from a word processor in that it is not designed for formatting text for printing.

Text-only format   Data saved in a format (typically by a word processor) that does not include any information about its formatting (such as character styles, margins, and so on). A Return appears at the end of each paragraph. This is the lowest-common denominator format that every word processor can read.

Text with line breaks   A variation on the Text-only format, the difference being that a Return character is placed at the end of every line, not just at the end of every paragraph. By saving text documents in this format, people with other kinds of computers see your original line breaks when they open the file.

Title bar   The top part of a window, showing the name of the document or folder being viewed. The title bar contains the Close and Zoom boxes, and the window can be moved on the screen by dragging its title bar.

Token Ring   A networking architecture developed by IBM. Macintoshes can connect to Token Ring networks when they are equipped with compatible interface boards and when a control panel called TokenTalk is installed.

Trash   The icon of a garbage can, located in the lower-right corner of the Finder screen. Files and folders dragged to the trash are deleted when you issue the Special menu Empty Trash command. Volumes dragged to the Trash are dismounted immediately.

True color   Refers to a monitor/interface card combination that can display 24-bit color (16 million+ colors). Supposedly, that number of colors is close enough to the number of colors that the human eye can distinguish as to create the illusion of reality.

TrueType   A method of describing fonts created by Apple for System 7 but now also used by Windows. Fonts in TrueType format will scale to other sizes on the screen, and produce smooth characters without the jaggies that appear when a bitmap-only font is scaled. TrueType fonts print well (if slowly) on PostScript printers, as well as QuickDraw printers.

Type 1 fonts   PostScript fonts. Fonts in this format are similar to TrueType fonts, in that they can be scaled correctly on the screen (providing Adobe Type Manger is present) and will also scale correctly on PostScript printers (with or without Adobe Type Manager).

Uploading   The act of transferring a file from a local computer to a distant one. (*See also* Downloading.)

User group   An organization (almost always non-profit) created to share information and expertise. Some groups, such as BMUG, specialize in the Mac. Others, such as the Boston Computer Society, cover all personal computers, but have a large and active Mac subgroup. User groups are an important resource for those who need solutions to difficult problems. They also usually maintain extensive libraries of non-commercial software. Many user groups also maintain libraries of commercial software for evaluation purposes.

Utility   A program that is not used for getting work done, *per se*, but is instead used to enhance the operation of the computer. Utilities do such things as compress or decompress files, help manage hard disks, back them up, and so on.

Virtual memory   A scheme by which a portion of the Mac's hard disk is used in such a way as to make the Macintosh think it has more RAM than it actually has. Virtual Memory in the Macintosh is enabled using the Memory control panel.

Virus   A program designed by computer terrorists to invade your computer unbeknownst to you. A few are less hostile than others; they may simply announce their presence, for example. Others, however, are designed to destroy your data. *See* Virus checkers.

Virus checkers   Programs that can 1) scan the files on a disk to determine whether or not they contain viruses or 2) reside in memory, watching for Virus-like activity.

Some programs also attempt to remove found viruses. While this sometimes works, if an application is infected with a virus the best way to remove the virus is to recopy the application from its original disk to the hard disk.

VM Storage   The invisible file created on your hard disk when you have enabled virtual memory. *See* Virtual memory.

Volume   Any disk, network volume, or partition that appears on the Macintosh desktop as a single disk.

Window   An area of the screen, defined by a title bar at the top and, usually, a scroll bar on the right, that is used to view the contents of a folder (in the Finder) or a document (in an application).

Word processor   A program used for typing, editing, formatting, and printing documents containing mostly text. Examples of this kind of document include letters, memos and manuscripts.

Zones   *See* Network zones.

Zoom box   The box on the right side of a window's title bar. Clicking this box expands the window to either 1) fill the screen or 2) make it large enough to hold its entire contents. Clicking the box again reverts it to its previous size.

Resources

The following list includes entries for products, companies, and individuals, and is organized alphabetically. Each product entry includes only the name of the company that sells it, while each company entry includes contact information as well as a list of the products it offers that are mentioned in this book. For the entries listed by an individual (shareware products are usually produced by an individual), the product is available from the usual shareware sources. These are electronic services such as CompuServe and America OnLine, BBS systems, and user groups. We hope to have made the list as current and complete as possible.

Access PC—Insignia Solutions Inc.

Addison Wesley Publishing Co.
  Jacob Way
  Reading, MA 01867
  Phone (617) 944-3700; Fax (617) 944-9338
    PowerBook Companion, 2nd Edition

Adobe PhotoShop—Adobe Systems Inc.

Adobe Systems Inc.
  1585 Charleston Rd.
  P.O. Box 7900
  Mountain View, CA 94039-7900
  Phone (415) 961-4400; Fax (415) 961-3769
    PhotoShop,
    ATM (Adobe Type Manager)
    PostScript

Adobe Type Manager (ATM)—Adobe Systems

Affinity Microsystems Ltd.
  1050 Walnut St., Suite 425
  Boulder, CO 80302
  Phone (303) 442-4840 or (800) 367-6771; Fax (303) 442-4999
    Tempo

Aladdin Systems Inc.
  165 Westridge Dr.
  Watsonville, CA 95076
  Phone (408) 761-6200; Fax (408) 761-6206
    Stuffit (Deluxe, Lite, Expander)

Alki Software Corp.
  300 Queen Anne Ave. N., Suite 410
  Seattle, WA 98109
  Phone (206) 286-2600 or (800) 669-9679; Fax (206) 286-2785
    Alki Seek

Alverson, David P.
  5635 Cross Creek Ct.
  Mason, OH 45040
    ZTerm

America OnLine Inc.
  8619 Westwood Center Dr.
  Vienna, VA 22182
  Phone (800) 827-6364
    America Online

AOCE (Apple Open Collaboration Environment)—Apple Computer

APDA—Apple Programmer's and Developer's Association
  Phone (800) 282-2732

Apple Computer Inc.
  20525 Mariani Ave.
  Cupertino, CA 95014
  Phone (408) 996-1010; Fax (408) 996-0275
    AppleLink
    AppleScript
    ARA (AppleTalk Remote Access)
    PC Exchange
    QuickTime Starter Kit

Apple Open Collaboration Environment (AOCE)—Apple Computer Inc.

ATM, Adobe Type Manager—Adobe Systems Inc.

Berkeley Mac Users Group—see BMUG Inc.

Berkeley Systems
  2095 Rose
  Berkeley, CA 94709
  Phone (510) 540-5535; Fax (510) 540-5115
    After Dark
    ScreenKeys
    Stepping Out

Bernoulli drives, cartridges- Iomega Corp

BMUG, Inc.
  1442 A Walnut St. #62
  Berkeley, CA 94709
  Phone (510) 549-2684; Fax (510) 849-9026

BookEndz—Pilot Technology

Boston Computer Society (BCS)
  48 Grove St. Davis Square
  Somerville, MA 02144
  Phone (617) 625-7080

Capture—Mainstay

Carbon Copy Mac—Microcom Software Systems

Casa Blanca Works (CK)
  148 Bon Air Ctr.
  Greenbrae, CA 94904
  Phone (415) 461-2227; Fax (415) 461-2249
    Drive7
    DriveShare

CE Software Inc.
  P.O. Box 65580
  1801 Industrial Circle
  West Des Moines, IA 50265
  Phone (515) 224-1995; Fax (515) 224-4534
    QuicKeys
    QuickMail

CIS—see Compuserve Information Service

Claris Corp.
  5201 Patrick Henry Dr.
  Box 58168
  Santa Clara, CA 95052
  Phone (408) 727-8227
    ClarisWorks
    FileMaker Pro II
    MacDraw
    MacProject
    MacWrite II
    Power to Go
    Resolve
    RetrieveIt

ClarisWorks—Claris Corp.

Coactive Computing Corp.
  1301 Shoreway Rd., Suite 221
  Belmont, CA 94002
  Phone (415) 802-1080; Fax (415) 593-9304
    Coactive Connector

Coactive Connector—Coactive Computing Corp.

Compact Pro—Bill Goodman

Complete Undelete (part of 911 Utilities)—Microcom Software Division

Compuserve Inc.
  5000 Arlington Centre Blvd.
  P.O. Box 20212
  Columbus, OH 43220
  Phone (614) 457-8600 or (800) 848-8990; Fax (614) 457-0348

CompuServe Information Manager—Compuserve Inc.
  CompuServe Information Service (CIS)

CompuServe Navigator—Michael C. O'Connor

Connectix Corp.
  2655 Campus Dr.
  San Mateo, CA 94403

Phone (415) 571-5100 or (800) 950-5880; Fax (415) 571-5195
   CPU (Connectix PowerBook Utilities)
   HandOff (CK really Connectix?)
   Mac Memory Guide, The
   Maxima
   Mode 32
   Virtual

Contour Systems Inc.
   P.O. Box 1763
   Los Altos, CA 94023
   Phone (415) 941-1000; Fax (415) 941-1474
      MouseTopper

CPU (Connectix PowerBook Utilities)—Connectix Inc.

CPU 2.0—Connectix Corp.

Dantz Development Corp.
   1400 Shattuck Ave., Suite 1
   Berkeley, CA 94709
   Phone (510) 849-0293; Fax (510) 849-1708
      DiskFit
      Network DiskFit
      Retrospect

DataViz Inc.
   55 Corporate Dr.
   Trumbull, CN 06611
   Phone (203) 268-0030; Fax (203) 268-4345
      MacLinkPlus

Dayna Communications Inc.
   Sorenson Research Park
   849 West Levoy Dr.
   Salt Lake City, UT 84123-2544
   Phone (801) 269-7200; Fax (801) 269-7363
   DOSMounter

DeBabelizer—Equilibrium Technologies

Disinfectant—John Norstad

DiskFit—Dantz Development Corp.

DOSMounter—Dayna Communications Inc.

Drive7—Casa Blanca Works

DriveShare—Casa Blanca Works

Easy Play—Michael C. O'Connor

Equilibrium Technologies
  475 Gate Five Rd., Suite 225
  Sausalito, CA 94965
  Phone (415) 332-4343; Fax (415) 332-4433

Excel—Microsoft Corp.

Farallon Computing Inc.
  2470 Mariner Square Loop
  Alameda, CA 94501-1010
  Phone (510) 814-5100; Fax (510) 814-5020
    PhoneNet connectors
    PhoneNet PC
    Timbuktu
    Timbuktu for Windows

FAXstf—STF Technologies Inc.

Fifth Generation Systems
  10049 N. Reiger Rd.
  Baton Rouge, LA 70809
  Phone (504) 291-7221
    Suitcase II

FileMaker Pro II—Claris Corp.

FileRunner—MBS Technologies

FindPro—ZiffNet/Mac

FlashIt—Nobu Toge

FWB Inc.
  2040 Polk St., Suite 215
  San Francisco, CA 94109
  Phone (415) 474-8055; Fax (415) 775-2125
    Hard Disk ToolKit

GCC Technologies
  580 Winter St.
  Waltham, MA 02154
  Phone (617) 890-0880 or (800) 422-7777; Fax (617) 890-0822
    WriteMove II

GifConverter—Kevin Mitchell

Global Village Communications Inc.
  685 E. Middlefield Rd., Building B
  Mountain View, CA 94043
  Phone (415) 390-8200 or (800) 736-4821; Fax (415) 390-8282
    PowerPort modems
    TelePort modems

GoFer—Microlytics Corp.

Goodman, Bill—Compact Pro

HandOff—Connectix Corp.

Hard Disk ToolKit—FWB Inc.

Hess, Robert—Shaman

Inline Design—PB Tools

Inline Sync—Inline Design

Insignia Solutions Inc.
  526 Clyde Ave.
  Mountain View, CA 94043
  Phone (415) 694-7600 or (800) 848-7677; Fax (415) 964-5434
    Access PC

Iomega Corp.
  1821 West 4000 South
  Roy, UT 84067
  Phone (801) 778-3000; Fax (801) 778-3460
    Bernoulli cartridge drives

Leader Technologies Inc.
  2964 Oceanside Blvd., Suite D
  Oceanside, CA 92054
  Phone (619) 721-7000; Fax (619) 721-4758
    PowerMerge

LetterPerfect—WordPerfect Corp.

Lind D-cell battery pack—Lind Electronic Design

Lind Electronic Design Inc.
  6414 Cambridge St.
  Minneapolis, MN 55426
  Phone (800) 659-5956 or (612) 927-6303; Fax (612) 927-7746
    Lind D-cell battery pack

Mac Memory Guide, The—Connectix Corp.

MacBinary

MacDraw Pro—Claris Corp.

MacLan Connect—Miramar Systems Inc.

MacLinkPlus—DataViz Inc.

MacRecorder—MacroMedia

MacroMedia
  600 Townsend St., Suite 310 West
  San Francisco, CA 94103
  Phone (415) 252-2000 or (800) 288-4797; Fax (415) 626-0554
    Director
    MacRecorder

MacSEE—(shareware) REEVEsoft

MacUser
  950 Tower Ln., 18th Floor
  Foster City, CA 94404
  Phone (415) 378-5600; Fax (415 378-6903
  Subscriptions (800) 627-2247

MacWEEK
  301 Howard St., 15th Floor
  San Francisco, CA 94105
  Phone (415) 243-3500; Fax (415)243-3650
  Subscriptions:
  c/o JCI
  P.O. Box 1766
  Riverton, NJ 08077
  Phone (609) 461-2100

MacWorld
  501 Second St.
  San Francisco, CA 94107
  Phone (415) 243-0505; Fax (415) 442-0766
  Subscriptions (800) 288-6848

Magic Typist—Tactic Software

Mannesmann Tally
  8301 South 180th St.
  Kent, WA 98032
  Phone (206) 251-5500; Fax (206) 251-5520
    MOBILEWriterPS

MasterSoft Inc. (Software ToolWorks)
  6991 E. Camelback Rd., Suite A-320
  Scottsdale, AZ 85251
  Phone (602) 277-0900; Fax (602) 970-0706
    Word for Word

MBS Technologies
  4017 Washington Rd., Suite 4000
  McMurry, PA 15317
  Phone (800) 860-8700 or (412) 941-9076; Fax (412) 941-7076
    FileRunner

McIntyre Computer Systems
  22809 Shagbark
  Birmingham, MI 48025
  Phone (313) 645-5090; Fax (313) 645-6042
    WordWriter

Microcom Software Division
  500 River Ridge Rd.
  Hatboro, MA 02062
  Phone (617) 551-1000; Fax (617) 551-1968
    911 Utilities
    Carbon Copy Mac

Microlytics Corp.
  Two Tobey Village Office Park
  Pittsford, NY 14534
  Phone (716) 248-9150; Fax (716) 248-3868
    GOfer

Microsoft Corp.
  1 Microsoft Way
  Redmond, WA 98052-6399
  Phone (206) 882-8080; Fax (206) 936-7329
    Excel
    Word

Microsoft Word—see Word

Microtech International Inc.
  158 Commerce St.
  East Haven, CN 06512
  Phone (203) 468-6223; Fax (203) 468-6466
    RAM (PowerBook SIMMs)

Miramar Systems Inc.
   201 N. Salsipuedes, Suite 204
   Santa Barbara, CA 93103
   Phone (805) 966-2432; Fax (805) 965-1824
      MacLan Connect

MOBILEWriterPS—Mannesmann Tally

Motion Works International Inc.
   1020 Mainland St, Suite 130
   Vancouver, BC, V6B 2T4
   Canada
   Phone (604) 685-9975; Fax (604) 685-6105
      Promotion

MouseTopper—Contour Systems Inc.

Newer Technology
   7803 E. Osie, Suite 105
   Wichita, KS 67207
   Phone (316) 685-4904 or (800) 678-3726; Fax (316) 685-9368
      RAM (PowerBook SIMMs)

Norton Essentials for the PowerBook—Symantec Corp.

Norton Utilities for the Macintosh—Symantec Corp.

Now Software Inc.
   319 S.W. Washington St. 11th Floor
   Portland, OR 97204
   Phone (503) 274-2800; Fax (503) 274-0670
      SuperBoomerang (part of Now Utilities)

Now Utilities—Now Software Inc.

On the Road—Palomar Software Inc.

Palomar Software Inc.
   2964 Oceanside Blvd., Suite D
   Oceanside, CA 92054
   Phone (619) 721-7000; Fax (619) 721-4758
      On the Road

PBTools—Inline Design

PhoneNet connectors—Farallon Computing Inc.

PhoneNet PC—Farallon Computing Inc.

Pilot Technology
   10025 Valley View Rd., Suite 130
   Eden Prairie, MN 55344
   Phone (800) 682-4987 or (612) 828-6002; Fax (612) 828-6806
      BookEndz

Pixel Flipper—Chris Sanchez

Power to Go—Claris Corp.

PowerBook Companion, 2nd Edition—Addison Wesley Publishing Co.

PowerMerge—Leader Technologies

PowerPort modem—Global Village Communications Inc.

PowerSwap—Utilitron

Prodigy
   445 Hamilton Ave.
   White Plains, NY 10601
   Phone (800) 776-3449

Promotion—Motion Works International Inc.

Qdea
   6331 Hilton Court
   Pine Springs, MN 55115
   Phone (800) 933-9558 or (612) 779-0955
      Synchronize

QuicKeys—CE Software Inc.

QuickMail—CE Software Inc.

QuickTime—Apple Computer Inc.

QuickTime Starter Kit—Apple Computer Inc.

RAM (PowerBook SIMMs)—Chip Merchant, Microtech, Newer Technology

RetrieveIt—Claris Corp.

Retrospect—Dantz Developement Corp.

SAM—see Symantec Anti-Virus Utilities

Sanchez, Chris—PixelFlipper

ScreenKeys—Berkeley Systems

Shaman—Robert Hess

Software Bridge for the Macintosh—Systems Compatibility Corp.

SonicPro International Inc.
    5201 Great America Parkway
    Santa Clara, CA 95954
    Phone (408) 982-2568; Fax (408) 982-2570
        SonicPro PowerBook Alarm

SonicPro PowerBook Alarm—SonicPro International Inc.

STF Technologies Inc.
    P.O. Box 81
    Concordia, MO 64020
    Phone (816) 463-2021; Fax (816) 463-2179
        FAXstf

Stuffit—Aladdin Systems Inc.

Suitcase II—Fifth Generation Systems

SuperBoomerang, Now Utilities—Now Software

SuperMac Technology
    485 Potrero Ave.
    Sunnyvale, CA 94086
    Phone (408) 245-2202; Fax (408) 735-7250
        VideoSpigot

Symantec Anti-Virus Utilities (SAM)—Symantec Corp.

Symantec Corp.
  10201 Torre Ave.
  Cupertino, CA 95014
  Phone (408) 253-9600 or (800) 441-7234; Fax (408) 252-4694
    GreatWorks
    Norton Essentials for the PowerBook
    Norton Utilities for the Macintosh
    Symantec Anti-Virus Utilities (SAM)

Synchronize—Odea

Systems Compatibility Corp.
  401 North Wabase, Suite 600
  Chicago, IL 60611
  Phone (312) 329-0700; Fax (312) 670-0820
    Software Bridge for the Macintosh

Tactic Software
  1617 North Flagler Dr., Suite 10B
  West Palm Beach, FL 33407-6506
    Magic Typist

TelePort modem—Global Village Communications Inc.

Tempo—Affinity Microsystems Ltd.

ThinPack external battery—VST Power Systems Inc.

Timbuktu—Farallon Computing Inc.

Timbuktu for Windows—Farallon Computing Inc.

Toge, Nobu—FlashIt

UnMount It—Apple

Utilitron
  6079 Madara Dr.
  Woodland Hills, CA 91367
  Phone (818) 883-4606; no Fax
    PowerSwap

VideoSpigot—SuperMac Technology

Virtual—Connectix Corp.

VST Power Systems Inc.
  1620 Sudbury Rd., Suite 3
  Concord, MA 01742
  Phone (508) 287-4600
    ThinPack external battery

Well, the
  27 Gate 5 Rd.
  Sausalito, CA 94965-1401
  Phone (415) 332-4335; Fax (415) 332-4927

Word—Microsoft Corp.

Word for Word—MasterSoft Inc. (Software ToolWorks)

WordPerfect Corp.
  1555 N. Technology Way
  Orem, UT 84057
  Phone (801) 225-5000; Fax (801) 228-5077
    LetterPerfect
    WordPerfect Mac
    WordPerfect Works

WordWriter—McIntyre Computer Systems

WriteMove II—GCC Technologies

ZiffNet/Mac
  950 Tower Ln.
  Foster City, CA 94404
  Phone (415) 578-6820; Fax (415) 578-6999
    FindPro

ZTerm—David Alverson

Index

All references are to tip numbers.

P

PackIt, 194
Parameter RAM, *see* PRAM
partitioning, hard disk, 258-261
    and PowerBook, 359
    and virtual memory, 259
    drawbacks, 258
passwords, 179
pasting, in dialog boxes, 281
PC Exchange, 202
PCs, 195, 202
performance, and defragmentation, 248
Photo-JPEG compressor, 122
PhotoShop, 194
PICT files, 194, 209
    JPEG compression, 125
PICTShow, 116
pit filename extension, 194
pkg filename extension, 194
PMMU, 221
Popcorn, 116
postponing printing, 145
PowerBooks
    and battery life, 343, 345
    and deferred FAXing, 353
    and deferred printing, 353
    and docking, 365, 367
    and external video, 361
    and file security, 367
    and Memory Control Panel, 233
    and memory upgrades, 360
    and second AC adaptor, 351
    and sleeping, 345, 370
    and swapping batteries, 350
    and VGA monitors, 362
    caring for batteries, 354
    backing up, 369
    choosing applications for, 313
    Enablers for, 217
    file synchronization, 372
    PowerBook Companion, 373

    support from Apple, 271
    utility software, 352
PowerMerge, 372
PRAM
    settings, 269
    zapping, 268
preference files, 69
Preferences folder, 80
print drivers, 141
printers, portable, 364
printing
    and PowerBook, 353
    background printing, 142, 143
    built-in, 157
    delaying printing, 145
    driver versions, 150
    fonts, downloading, 155
    kinds of printers, 148
    LaserPrinter driver 8.0, 151, 152
    postponing printing, 145
    PostScript files with version 7.0 driver, 153
    PostScript files with version 8.0 driver, 154
    print drivers, 141
PrintMonitor, 144, 145, 147
Prodigy, 190
Program Linking, defined, 172
ProMotion, 111
publish and subscribe, 302
Put Away Command
    and Networks, 181
    to eject floppy disks, 21

Q

Quadras, Enablers for, 217
QuickDraw GX, 140
QuicKeys, 134, 231, 285, 335
QuickTime, 231
    acquiring, 109
    CD audio tracks, 117
    compressors, 122
    converting system sound to movie, 121